The Light at the Top of the Mountain

...*Ghosts in the Bible*

Mitchel Whitington

ISBN 978-1-9393060-2-9

Library of Congress Control Number: 2013922583

Printed in the United States of America
Published by 23 House Publishing
SAN 299-8084
www.23house.com

A Dedication

I was raised in an environment where asking any questions about God and religion was forbidden – almost heresy, in fact. In that world, heavy, unmovable walls are constructed around everyone to protect their thoughts, and anything beyond those walls was considered either untrue or evil. At some point in my life, however, I discovered that there is an incredible, supernatural world that is very much a part of our reality, but it lies just outside the walls that most of us cling to so tightly.

I have been fortunate in my life to have encountered many mentors; some taught me by holding onto and espousing absolute untruths, others by being willing to debate and discuss the various aspects of religion and the nature of God Himself. I found that life is a journey of discovery, and that it begins when the walls are finally torn down, and you allow yourself to explore.

I've come to believe that God doesn't want us to blindly follow the rules and dogma set forth by man, but instead, to look to his true essence, exemplified by the teachings of Christ while he was on Earth. This book is therefore dedicated to my mentors – some that have no idea what impact they've had on me, and others who continue to be an integral part of my everyday life. Without guides along the way, life's journey would not be possible.

Table of Contents

Behold, I show you a mystery; we shall not all sleep, but we shall all be changed.
– 1 Corinthians 15:51

That the dead appear to the living in any way whatever is by the special dispensation of God, in order that the souls of the dead may interfere in affairs of the living – and this is to be accounted as miraculous.
– Saint Thomas Aquinas

Section 1: A Few Words from the Author

I've been writing this book, oh, probably for a decade now... but without knowing it. It's just that my interest in the supernatural goes back to my childhood, and I've spent a lifetime with friends and relatives telling me that contemplating such things was "evil" or "of Satan." It was to the point that I sometimes hid my interests for fear of what people might think of me.

The more that I studied the scriptures, however, the more that I became convinced that what I was being told by people was simply not the entire truth – that the world just behind the veil from ours is not only very real, but is a major part of God's creation as well. I found that the Bible not only speaks freely about it, but it seems to beckon us to remove the walls from around us and enjoy the full world that God had created for us.

I kept notes over the years – Bibles passages, references to commentaries on the scripture, accounts of my own experiences, etc... until at one point, I realized that I had quite a bit of information. Not being one to hide my candle under a bushel, I felt compelled to share the things that I had come to know.

I should be quick to say that I am a Christian – probably more by my own standards than the world's. Instead of being a part of an organized religion with rules and dogma set forth by man, I instead humbly try to follow the teachings of Jesus while he was on Earth.

The Bible is full of laws given by God at different times to different people for different reasons. To decide that every single one applies to our world today is ludicrous. In the town where I live, for example, I've been told that there is a law still on the books prohibiting you from riding your horse down a sidewalk. It's definitely not something that we need today, but back in the 1800s when everyone traveled by horseback it was probably a huge safety issue. And so it is with some the Bible's rules.

Yet some people treat the Bible like a buffet, choosing the laws that they will obey and judge others by, while dismissing the laws that don't fit their current needs or life for one reason or another.

As we go forward, let me make one more thing very, very clear. I'm not claiming to be an expert on the Bible, and it's not my intent to tell you what you should or shouldn't believe. Although I've been reading and studying it for most of my life, I continue to marvel at what is clearly much, much more than just an ordinary book.

I greatly encourage you to have the Bible out while you're reading this book. Look up every scripture and read it for yourself.

I would ask that you study everything, draw your own conclusions, and use this book not as a definitive word on the subject, but instead a springboard for your own research.

The Bible is a paradox, both very simple and very complex at the same time… and it is as wonderful as our Universe is.

The Three Premises of this Book

There are just a few basic premises that I want to mention before getting too far along, just so we're on the same page; they're the constructs by which this book is written, if you will. Any of them could be the topic of their own book, and as such, I want to just acknowledge them right up front so as not to spend a lot of time hashing them over later. Just as there are rules to the game of baseball, these are kind of the ground rules for this book. There are those who will disagree with them, which is perfectly fine, but at least for the purposes of going forward we'll be in agreement as to the context of the material.

Premise One: The Bible is the divine Word of God

As a Christian, I believe this to be absolutely true. It's not something that I just blindly accept, however; over the years it has been an inspiration and a guide for me. Scriptures have lifted me up when I was down, given me comfort when I was afraid, and provided inspiration in ways that I could never have imagined. With all the things that people claim that the Bible is – and isn't – I know that the Bible is the inspired word of God.

Another complete volume could be written containing arguments for and against that fact, but that's not what we are here to discuss for the purposes of this book.

3

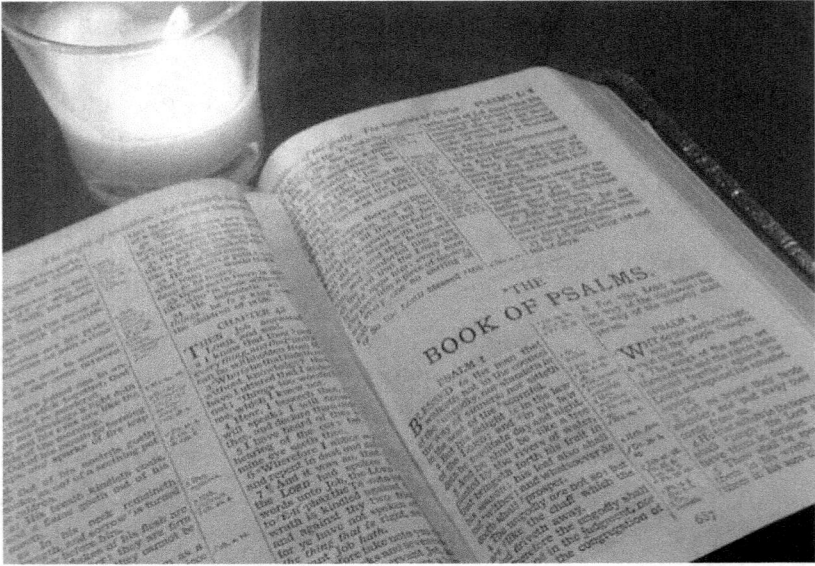

Premise Two: The Bible is God's Word, and it is meant for all people

By that, I mean that you don't have to be a monk sequestered in a monastery who's spent his entire life transcribing Hebrew (or Greek, or Aramaic, or whatever) scrolls to understand the Bible. If the Bible is truly the Word of God, which I believe that it is, then He must have given it to us all: the guy with a sixth-grade education, eating a bologna sandwich sitting on his tractor and reading it during a lunch break in the hay field, as much as a learned Catholic Monsignor who's spent his life in the service of God at the Vatican. I call this premise my *guy-on-a-tractor* rule, which I'll be referring to several times later in the book. This is more of a problem than you might think, because often when I'm talking about the Bible, someone will say something to me like, "You can't make that statement, because if you look back to the

4

original Hebrew (or Greek, or Aramaic), this particular word actually means…"

Not knowing any ancient languages myself, I would have to take that person's word for it. But if we are to rely on others who do know the ancient language of the Scriptures to tell us what one particular word or phrase means, then aren't we opening ourselves up to their particular interpretation, instead of letting the Word of God speak directly to us? And to make matters worse, most people don't read the ancient languages and haven't read the original scrolls, so they are getting the translations from another source, which might be quoting yet another source – the information might have gone through several people, and be third- or forth-hand… or worse. I prefer to let the Word of God speak to me.

The average "guy on the tractor," who should be able to read and understand the Word of God, at least in my estimation

I was attending a church service one Sunday morning, and the pastor held up his Bible and said, "This is the Word of God, and I'm tired of people trying to interpret it. It doesn't need interpretation!" About ten minutes later into the sermon, he read a verse and said, "Now let me tell you what that means…" I wanted to stand up and ask, "Hang on a minute – aren't you interpreting that verse?"

I don't know… I have a hard time with such things. If God meant for the average Joe to have to learn a foreign language, travel to a Middle Eastern university, and peruse the original scrolls to understand the Bible, then I'd argue whether God was taking it seriously or not.

But when it comes to the Bible itself, I'm banking on the fact that you or I can stroll into the local bookstore, pick up one of the popular translations, and use it to see what God has to say to us.

And speaking of different versions of the Bible, It's kind of strange to me that all the different translations are literally owned by one company or another. They're copyrighted material – the Word of God is literally owned by man.

The King James Version is in public domain, which is why that's all you see quoted in this book. If I was going to use another translation in this book, I would have to get permission of the corporation that is the owner of the Word of God (at least, that version) and perhaps even pay them for the privilege of doing so. Or even more likely, if they disagreed with my using the Scripture to investigate the subject of ghosts, they could get an injunction against me publishing (and therefore you reading) this book. How weird is that?

It even gets a little stranger, though. In the United

Kingdom, even the King James Version (KJV) is copyrighted. Case in point: when that translated version was 400 years old, the Globe Theater (Shakespeare's old stomping ground) was going to honor that occasion by having a series of actors read the entire Bible on stage start to finish, Genesis to Revelation, culminating on Easter Sunday 2011. According to *BBC Music Magazine*, a few days before the event the production company received a substantial bill for performing copyrighted material – the Word of God. In the U.K., the Royal Crown owns the copyright to the King James Version of the Bible, and has since King James himself had it done... the Queen wanted to be paid for it!

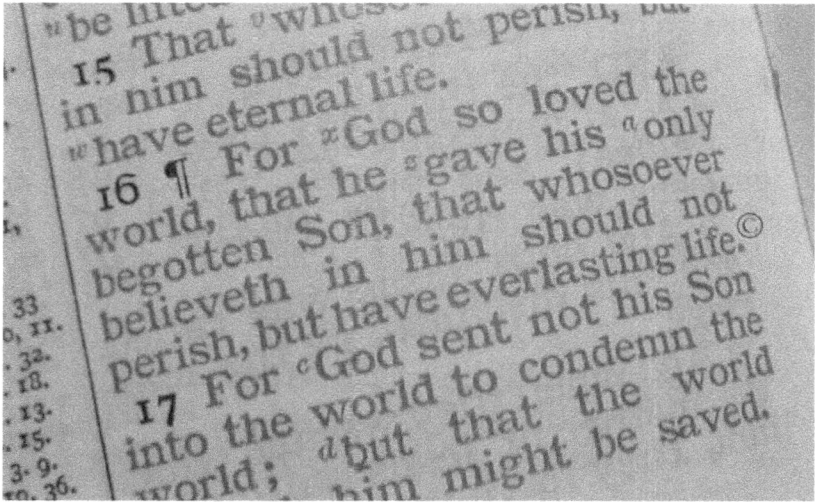

Okay, not a real photo... but it does make you think, right?

Outside of the U.K. the King James Version of the Bible is public domain, so presumably I won't be hearing from the Queen for quoting it here, and to be honest I'm not really worried.

Premise Three: There are more things in heaven and earth, Horatio, than are dreamt of in your philosophy.

Shakespeare penned those words in Hamlet, Act 1, Scene 5, where the characters were discussing the appearance of a ghost. The third premise that I'm going to state is pretty simple: ghosts exist, along with a lot of other things outside of the realm of what science understands today... the same science that once held true that the Earth was flat, and later after a bit of enlightenment, that the entire universe revolved around the Earth.

Stories of spirits returning after death permeate every culture through history. Not scary, fictional tales around a campfire, but encounters with the supernatural by sane, rational people.

The *Epic of Gilgamesh* is an epic poem from Mesopotamia, and it is amongst the earliest surviving works of literature, dating all the way back to the 17th century B.C. In the story, Gilgamesh is conversing with the spirit of his dead friend Enkidu.

In Egypt, Limestone tablets dating to 1200 B.C. record the story of Nebusemekh, a wealthy man who died but whose spirit appeared to the high priest of Amun-Re.

Homer, who lived around the 7th or 8th centuries B.C. included ghosts in his epic tales of the *Iliad* and the *Odyssey*, and you'll also find spirits in Shakespeare's *Hamlet* and *Macbeth*.

In the United States of America, which at the age of 200+ years is a relative newcomer to the history of the world, no less than six of our presidents have reported encountering ghosts in the White House – not crackpots, but leaders of the free world! Winston Churchill, the esteemed Prime Minister of England, encountered one while staying there, as did Queen Wilhelmina of the Netherlands.

Could the spirit of Old Abe be walking those hallways?

Forget about famous encounters, though – on a more down-home note, I'd bet that there isn't anyone you know that doesn't have at least one friend or relative that has had an encounter with the supernatural. The staunchest non-believers will hang their head in embarrassment and admit that they have a loved one who believes in the supernatural.

A CBS News poll conducted in 2009 revealed that 48% of Americans believe in ghosts, while 45% do not. The other 7% were undecided. Interestingly enough, 22% of Americans say that they have seen or felt the presence of a ghost – that's one in every five people.

Personally, I know that ghosts are real – they do exist, and I don't feel the need to debate it with someone who doesn't. You see, if that person and I were to travel to China and stand in front of the Great Wall, it would be foolish of me to stand there and say, "That wall isn't real. It's a figment of our imagination. It's our mind playing tricks on us. It really doesn't exist." That person would think me mad. But that's exactly what I'd be doing if I were to say that ghosts don't exist, because I have personally experienced them. Denying that fact does not alter their existence at all. They are there, whether we choose to believe in them or not… just as the Great Wall of China is.

It's all right, though; people tell me that they don't believe in ghosts, which is absolutely fine with me. I know a fellow who doesn't believe that man landed on the moon, that it was all filmed on a Hollywood sound stage just so that we would win the "space race" against the Communist Ruskies. That idea got enough steam behind it to inspire a Hollywood movie. Another person I'm acquainted with doesn't believe that John F. Kennedy was really assassinated – that he was merely wounded, and they were able to keep him alive. The theory gets even stranger, involving the idea that Jackie Kennedy married the bizillionaire Aristotle Onassis so that she would have the money to keep JFK alive at a secret facility away from the U.S. on some island somewhere. What a person does or does not believe is up to them and is something that they have to resolve in their own mind. After all, it's a free country.

The third premise that this books starts with, however is that ghosts exist. Other books can debate that fact – here we're just going to be concerned with what the Bible has to say on the subject... so let's get started!

Section 2: The Problem with Religion and Ghosts

Things have become a little strange in our world. You see, some of my fondest childhood memories are of Halloween, when my grade-school friends would dress up in costumes of skeletons, ghosts and witches, all meet at my house, and then go trick-or-treating around the neighborhood. We knew everyone at every house, there was never a thought of danger, and my parents didn't even follow us to keep us safe – there was no need.

As a teenager, the church that I attended always had a big Halloween celebration, staging elaborate "haunted houses" for the kids of the city to walk through for a scare, complete with vampires and monsters of all types. There would be horror movies shown in the Fellowship Hall of the church, and of course, lots of popcorn and candy.

Somewhere along the way, though, Christianity took the supernatural to task, deciding that it was all evil inspired by the very hand of Satan. Horror movies were condemned, and Halloween "haunted houses" were taboo unless they'd been "sanitized" by the church so that the scary scenes reflected abortion, drug and alcohol use, and of course going to hell because you weren't saved – that is to say, you weren't a member of the particular host church.

Trick-or-treaters reveling at Halloween

I'm not sure when – or why – this giant u-turn in thinking happened, but it did. It's not just Halloween, though. Anytime the subject of the supernatural is broached, it is immediately condemned by most "religious" groups.

More than one person has directly said that the books that I've written on the supernatural are downright evil, which, I guess, would mean that I'm evil as well!

One day when my mother was in the hospital, at

14

death's door from a blood clot that had moved from her leg to her heart, I was sitting in the waiting room while she was being attended to in intensive care. A pastor came to check on her, and sat down out in the waiting room for a while since he couldn't go in to see her. Making small talk I suppose, he said, "So I understand that you live in a haunted house…"

I smiled politely and replied that we do have our share of supernatural activity at The Grove.

He then said, "Well, that's not Biblical, you know."

I would have loved to debate him, but at the time I was too concerned about my mother to care what he said. That did, however, led me to wonder even more just what the Bible says about ghosts.

After many years of hearing them from people firsthand, here are some of the things that are quoted by those who believe that supernatural happenings are wicked... at least, according to the Bible.

A Quick Look at the Bible and Ghosts

What does the Bible have to say about people who try to communicate with ghosts? Here's Isaiah 8:19 on the subject:

[19]*And when they shall say unto you, Seek unto them that have familiar spirits, and unto wizards that peep, and that mutter: should not a people seek unto their God? for the living to the dead?*

So as it says, if someone suggests that you consult mediums who whisper and mutter to the spirit world, you should instead turn to God. It goes on to ask why in the world you would consult the dead on behalf of the living.

But what about those people to try to actively communicate with spirits, as many ghost hunters do? Leviticus 19:31 talks about this very clearly:

31Regard not them that have familiar spirits, neither seek after wizards, to be defiled by them: I am the Lord your God.

So it says not to seek out anyone who is involved with spirits, or you will be corrupted by them.

There are places that are reputed to be very active with the supernatural – haunted houses and buildings, for example. What does the Bible say about them? The book of Job covers that in chapter 7, where verses 9 and 10 say:

9As the cloud is consumed and vanisheth away: so he that goeth down to the grave shall come up no more.
10He shall return no more to his house, neither shall his place know him any more.

That clearly states that when someone dies and is put in a grave, he won't be seen again. He doesn't get to return to his house – his home won't know him anymore.

There are some folks that claim to have received a message from a dead loved one; is that possible? Not according to Ecclesiastes 9:5-6.

5For the living know that they shall die: but the dead know not any thing, neither have they any more a reward; for the memory of them is forgotten.
6Also their love, and their hatred, and their envy, is

now perished; neither have they any more a portion for ever in any thing that is done under the sun.

That says that the living know that they're going to die, but the dead don't know anything. They don't have any more of a reward, and all memory of them is eventually forgotten. All emotion is gone as well – love, hate, jealousy, it is all gone. The Book of Psalms, Chapter 115:16-17, shows that the dead don't even praise the Lord:

[16]*The heaven, even the heavens, are the Lord's: but the earth hath he given to the children of men.*
[17]*The dead praise not the Lord, neither any that go down into silence.*

You sometimes hear about people who have died with unfinished business in life, and they come back as spirits to resolve the issues. Psalm 146:4 speaks against that, though:

[4]*His breath goeth forth, he returneth to his earth; in that very day his thoughts perish.*

So as the Psalm says, when your final breath leaves your body, you will decay back into the Earth, and all of your thoughts are gone.

All of the verses listed in this section make a strong case using the Bible that ghosts can't be the spirits of departed humans.

Christian author Ron Rhodes, writing in his book *The Truth Behind Ghosts, Mediums, and Psychic Phenomena,* observes, "People sometimes genuinely encounter a spirit entity – though not a dead human. Some people encounter demonic spirits who may mimic dead people in order to deceive the living. Many who claim to have encountered such entities have some prior involvement in the occult." He supports his words with 1 John 4:1, which says:

¹Beloved, believe not every spirit, but try the spirits whether they are of God: because many false prophets are gone out into the world.

Such are the things that you'll hear over and over again concerning the Bible and ghosts, and those are just a few – there are certainly more. If these were the final words on the subject, though, there would be no need for this book. So there are clearly a few more things to say, and I'll start with a few personal thoughts.

One Christian's View of Ghosts

I feel like I'm walking a tightrope as I write this book – not wanting to offend anyone on one hand, while seeking the truth on the other.

Once I started looking into the Biblical view of ghosts, the reason that I continued down the road of researching the subject became a little personal. When I was researching and writing the book *Ghosts of North Texas*, a member of my family thought that I had crossed over into the realm of demons and evil. That person who was so dear to me sent Bible verses with commentary to show what a sinful endeavor I was entering into.

But writing that book wasn't the start of my interest in the supernatural – that has been part of my life for as far

18

back as I can remember. My first recollection of actually voicing that interest was all the way back in the first grade.

My teacher, Mrs. Lola Reed, had passed out a line drawing of a chair, and asked that every student color his or her chair with a favorite crayon. Kids around me were using blues, greens, pinks, and a rainbow of other colors. As I stopped to think of what my favorite color would be, I went back to a mental image that I'd always had of an old house at twilight. Since the sun had set, the house itself was in silhouette, and was therefore very dark; black, in fact. I don't know where the image came from, but it had always been in my mind. I can close my eyes and see it today. The one thing that I knew about the house was that ghosts lived there, and for some reason that was comforting and secure to me. I therefore colored my chair black.

A haunted house image very similar to the one in my young mind

I didn't know that Mrs. Reed was going to put all the chair-pictures up for parent-teacher night at the elementary school, however. When my mother and dad took me to the classroom that evening, they found my picture, looked at it, and asked, "Why did you color your chair black?"

I simply said, "Because that's the color of haunted houses." In retrospect, I'm very lucky that they didn't put me right into therapy for showing signs of depression or something like that. Still, I remember that night like it was only yesterday – it was the first time that I remember voicing an interest in the supernatural aloud.

All my life I've walked that fine line, with a strong interest in the supernatural on one hand, but people that I love and respect on the other telling me that it's all evil and demonic. In the past I've struggled between this profound fascination with the other realms of our universe, and my own faith as I have been told that any exploration outside of the defined values of our denomination was immoral and wrong.

As I said before, I am a Christian… although sometimes that title bothers me. After all, some terrible, terrible things have been done over the years in the name of Christianity. A few hundred years ago, people were inhumanely tortured and persecuted in the name of the "Holy Inquisition." From Europe to America, women were accused of witchcraft and were either stoned, drowned, hanged, beheaded, or burned alive to purge the demons from them.

In the past decade or so, tele-evangelists have made claims – purportedly from God – that their cable TV congregation must send them money or horrible things would happen. Doomsday cults have committed mass suicide because their "prophet" claims to hear the voice of the Lord, and helpless children have been molested by other "religious" leaders who were supposedly the moral bastions of the church. Over the past few years, several mothers have taken the lives of their children because "God" told them to. When I consider how Christ must feel about all the things being done in his name, I think back to the scripture, specifically John 11:35, which simply says, *Jesus wept.*

But what does being a Christian mean to me? Well, I believe that Jesus Christ is the only and absolute Son of God, and that the Bible is the inspired Word of God.

While that might sound familiar, I have to tell you that there are people who might call my statement into question. You see, I also know that the world that we live in is filled with many, many things that are outside the boundaries of what most people deem to be natural. They are supernatural things, including ghosts, and they are as much a part of our world as you and I are.

Make no mistake – it's not that I'm simply choosing to think that ghosts exist. I've actually seen their forms, smelled their scents of perfume or cigar smoke, heard their rambling noises, even voices, and have experienced them with all of my senses. I've also written numerous articles and books on the subject of the supernatural over the years, and traveled to haunted places from literally one coast to the other. I've interviewed hundreds of people who have had many similar experiences, and so in my mind, there can be no question about the existence of these things that we call "spirits," "ghosts," or whatever moniker you want to hang on them.

21

One of the things that has solidified my beliefs is the fact that my wife and I live in an antebellum home built in 1861 known as "The Grove" in Jefferson, Texas, where the ghost stories go back over a hundred years. From the lady in the white dress that walks through the house, to the black-suited man in the garden, we've had supernatural encounters since we purchased the house back in 2002. Living in a "haunted" house – although I'm not a huge fan of that term – has taught me that it's not just that "ghosts" are real. Instead, I've come to understand that the world we live in is much broader that most of us ever imagine. It includes not only the "natural" things that we all accept, but the things beyond that as well... a realm that we call the "supernatural."

The Grove, Jefferson, Texas

My wife and I feel that we are truly blessed to live in a place with so much supernatural activity. To us it adds another dimension to our lives, but some people's reaction is strange. They mistakably assume that we live some kind of odd life like television's *Addams Family* or *The Munsters*.

It is a beautiful, historic home, and tours are given there on weekends. We tell both the history of the house and share some of its many ghost stories. More than once, someone has pointed to my Granddad's Bible that is on display in the parlor, and said something like, "Don't you have a conflict between having that out and then telling all these ghost stories?"

People can't reconcile the fact that as I'm relating some of our supernatural experiences, there is a Bible in the room – it's like the two things are mutually exclusive; at least, in their minds.

Another very common experience in my life is for someone to chuckle, get a humoring smile on their face, and say, "Well, I don't really believe in ghosts." They wait for an answer or a challenge from me, but I usually just shrug and go on. I've found that it's pointless to engage people in debate – if their mind is already made up, then there's probably no way I could ever change it… not that I'm even inclined to.

What really bothers me, though, is when someone tells me that the idea of ghosts is evil, or that believing in such things goes against the will or teachings of Christ. That calls into question my own spiritual convictions, and that is something that I have always have to consider, examine and reconcile in my own mind. And for that, I have to look to religion and the Bible.

Section 3: Obeying the Laws of the Bible

I can't really hold people at fault who crusade against the evils of ghosts and the supernatural; I think that their beliefs probably came about innocently enough. For the most part, someone at some point in their lives probably told them how evil the supernatural was, and then quoted a Bible verse such as Leviticus 19:31 to them:

³¹Regard not them that have familiar spirits, neither seek after wizards, to be defiled by them: I am the Lord your God.

Or perhaps a person heard about a verse in the Bible that actually carries the death sentence for such offences. There's nothing more fun than being able to accuse someone of a sin worthy of death. Leviticus 20:27 says:

²⁷A man also or woman that hath a familiar spirit, or that is a wizard, shall surely be put to death: they shall stone them with stones: their blood shall be upon them.

These verses get thrown up all the time as definitive proof that any involvement with the supernatural is evil, demonic, and wrong.

The Sorceress, Jan Van Der Velde, c. 1626

You have to be careful, however – if you're going to try to enforce those laws about ghosts, there are quite a few more that you should be aware of concerning other things that will be obligated to obey as well. You know, probably the best example I saw of this was a photograph of a gentleman who'd had a huge tattoo put on his arm – and I do mean huge, in very big letters – of the familiar Bible verse concerning homosexuality, Leviticus 18:22, which says:

Thou shalt not lie with mankind, as with womankind: it is abomination.

26

The tattooed fellow was clearly anti-gay, but taking such a drastic step... well, to paraphrase Shakespeare's *Hamlet*, Act III, scene II, *methinks he doth protest too much*. For whatever reason, though, he wanted to make sure that he got his message across to the world, so that everyone knew his stance... and probably so that he could feel more secure in his own manhood for whatever reason.

Unfortunately, he never realized that just a chapter later, Leviticus 19:28 says:

Ye shall not make any cuttings in your flesh for the dead, nor print any marks upon you: I am the LORD.

The same book of the Holy Bible that has a verse prohibiting homosexuality also prohibits tattoos, but I guess he simply didn't look far enough to see that... or like most people, had determined that one law should be followed to the letter because he agreed with it, while the other could be ignored because he didn't. This is the kind of thing that happens when man appoints himself custodian of God's Word.

There are a lot of laws to obey if you're going to head down the road of judging others, though. First of all, you can only eat sea creatures that have fins and scales, according to Leviticus 11:9-12:

[9]These shall ye eat of all that are in the waters: whatsoever hath fins and scales in the waters, in the seas, and in the rivers, them shall ye eat.
[10]And all that have not fins and scales in the seas, and in the rivers, of all that move in the waters, and of any

living thing which is in the waters, they shall be an abomination unto you:

[11]*They shall be even an abomination unto you; ye shall not eat of their flesh, but ye shall have their carcases in abomination.*

[12]*Whatsoever hath no fins nor scales in the waters, that shall be an abomination unto you.*

A buffet of seafood that Leviticus prohibits you from eating

Think that you're okay with this one? Well, if you go to any all-you-can-eat catfish buffet, you're wallowing in sin... because although catfish have fins they definitely don't have scales – instead they have skin. On the other hand, if you go to a crab restaurant and order Alaskan Snow Crab Legs, you violate this scripture as well – you're a sinner, at the magnitude of being a witch or someone who consorts with spirits by the standards of those who judge such things. If you've ever ordered a shrimp cocktail, well, don't even get me started.

According to Leviticus 19:19, it is forbidden by God to let one type of cattle breed with another. In the cattle industry today, this is not an uncommon practice. Breeds are mixed to produce genetically better cattle for beef. The industry staple *Beef Magazine* recently reported that beef-producing ranches today want cattle that are 50-75% Angus, up to 50% Continental, with no more than 25% Bos indicus or other breeds for the best product. These ranches, of course, are breaking Levitical law.

Now the big question becomes: how does that apply to all of us who purchase beef in the grocery store, without knowing whether it comes from cattle that has been cross-bred for quality? We are, after all supporting such a practice. Hmmm... definitely something to ponder.

Uh-oh... two Frisians and a Jersey grazing together

29

On a completely different topic, I do hope that you are avoiding "unclean women," that is to say, woman who are menstruating. This is mentioned several times in the scripture. For example, Leviticus 15:19 says:

19And if a woman have an issue, and her issue in her flesh be blood, she shall be put apart seven days: and whosoever toucheth her shall be unclean until the even.

That means that you must banish any women who are on their period, be it your wife, daughter, mother, office worker, boss... whoever she is. Just to make sure, I'd recommend asking the women that you encounter throughout the day whether or not they're menstruating so that you can avoid them if need be (okay, that was definitely tongue-in-cheek... such inquiries would get you some very rude comments, if not downright slapped). The "unclean" problem is more than just touching a woman in such a condition; if you are a woman and are on your period, then anything that *you* touch becomes "unclean" and no one else can touch that particular item. I'm sure that includes desks, computer keyboards, automobiles, grocery carts... you name it. Leviticus 20:18 reads:

18And if a man shall lie with a woman having her sickness, and shall uncover her nakedness; he hath discovered her fountain, and she hath uncovered the fountain of her blood: and both of them shall be cut off from among their people.

So if a man has sexual relations with a woman who is on her period, then both of them must be cut off from their people.

Of course, gentlemen, you can't cut your hair or beard, as prescribed in Leviticus 19:27, something we talked about earlier in the book. Remember the days when "hippies" grew their hair and beards long? Well, it turns out that they must have been much more pleasing in God's eyes than a Marine who goes to a barber and gets a buzz cut. If you're keeping the laws of Leviticus, and you're a guy, then going to the barber, in the eyes and judgment of God you are committing a sin.

Oh, and I hope that you've never said anything bad about your folks. Although we've all been mad at Mom or Dad at one time or another, check out Leviticus 20:9...

⁹*For every one that curseth his father or his mother shall be surely put to death: he hath cursed his father or his mother; his blood shall be upon him.*

That verse definitively says that any person who curses his mother or father must be killed.

The laws get worse. My neighbor has a small part of his yard where he has an annual garden that includes tomatoes, corn, cucumbers, and many other delectables. Who could have imagined that his innocent little garden would be an abomination in the eyes of God? Apparently it is, though. Leviticus 19:19 clearly states that you shouldn't have a variety of crops on the same field...

¹⁹*...thou shalt not sow thy field with mingled seed.*

Now that I think about it, I could be in some serious trouble myself. My wife and I once purchased a package of seeds at Wal Mart that was a combination of different types of wildflowers – once you sowed them into a flower bed it produced a rainbow garden... but the seeds were definitely mingled!

Like they say on TV commercials, "but wait... there's more!" It is forbidden for you to wear clothes that are made of more than one fabric – that's in Leviticus 19:19 as well:

[19]*Neither shall a garment mingled of linen and woolen come upon thee.*

This law is so important that it's mentioned again in Deuteronomy 22:11.

style/modele:sport coat
shell/exterieur

62% WOOL
25% LINEN
13% NYLON

lining\doublure:
100% viscose
RN: 84348

The tag from a garment that clearly violates Leviticus 19:19 and 22:11

If a man cheats on his wife, or vise versa, both the man and the woman involved in the infidelity must die, as prescribed by Leviticus 20:10. In our world today, that would actually include many politicians and preachers. There are even websites that exist for the sole purpose of helping people find hook-ups for affairs. Here's the verse:

[10]*And the man that committeth adultery with another man's wife, even he that committeth adultery with his neighbour's wife, the adulterer and the adulteress shall surely be put to death.*

All of our nation's handicap rights laws need to be modified so that they don't include churches. The house of God certainly doesn't need to be handicap accessible, because Leviticus 21:17-18 dictates:

[16]*And the LORD spake unto Moses, saying,*

[17]*Speak unto Aaron, saying, Whosoever he be of thy seed in their generations that hath any blemish, let him not approach to offer the bread of his God.*

[18]*For whatsoever man he be that hath a blemish, he shall not approach: a blind man, or a lame, or he that hath a flat nose, or any thing superfluous,*

[19]*Or a man that is brokenfooted, or brokenhanded,*

[20]*Or crookbackt, or a dwarf, or that hath a blemish in his eye, or be scurvy, or scabbed, or hath his stones broken;*

[21]*No man that hath a blemish of the seed of Aaron the priest shall come nigh to offer the offerings of the LORD made by fire: he hath a blemish; he shall not come nigh to offer the bread of his God.*

33

Most churches have handicapped parking, which is definitely unneeded according to Leviticus 21

Actually, this scripture causes a problem for me personally, because if you look at verse 20, it says that anyone who *hath a blemish in his eye* isn't fit to enter the House of God.

I wear glasses, so I guess that it would be wrong for me to go to church – because to do so would be to profane God's sanctuary (according to Leviticus). Hopefully people who wear glasses or contacts, or have any kind of visual defects aren't defiling the House of God by attending worship services. The only problem is, Leviticus doesn't tell us what to do with the offenders, so I'm not clear whether we should smite them or not. I vote that we err on the side of caution – let's not start indiscriminately killing eyeglass-wearing church-goers until we get a clearer ruling on this law.

Oh, and speaking of our country's laws, there needs to

be a repeal of any religious tolerance. In America you can pretty much worship as you choose. You can be a Christian, Buddhist, Pagan, Wicca, Jew, Scientologist, Muslim, agnostic, or even a down-right atheist, and your rights to believe as you choose will be constitutionally protected. Turns out that idea isn't Biblical at all. Deuteronomy 17:2 says,

²If there be found among you, within any of thy gates which the LORD thy God giveth thee, man or woman, that hath wrought wickedness in the sight of the LORD thy God, in transgressing his covenant,

³And hath gone and served other gods, and worshipped them, either the sun, or moon, or any of the host of heaven, which I have not commanded;

⁴And it be told thee, and thou hast heard of it, and enquired diligently, and, behold, it be true, and the thing certain, that such abomination is wrought in Israel:

⁵Then shalt thou bring forth that man or that woman, which have committed that wicked thing, unto thy gates, even that man or that woman, and shalt stone them with stones, till they die.

Basically, the Bible is decreeing the death sentence for anyone who doesn't follow the same religion that you do – although I guess that is under the assumption that your religion is the correct one in God's eyes. The only problem is figuring out exactly which religion gets to be the "right" one; I'm sure that any and all religions would insist that theirs be deemed as such, which adds to the confusion.

But it's not just the cosmic topics such as religion that

35

you have to worry about. Deuteronomy 22:5 gives women some basic rules for dressing:

> [5]*The woman shall not wear that which pertaineth unto a man, neither shall a man put on a woman's garment: for all that do so are abomination unto the Lord thy God.*

All right, ladies, if you happen to be wearing pants, shorts or a smart business suit, look out – in God's eyes, you're an abomination! A popular trend in young ladies' apparel lately has been to wear cowboy boots with a skirt – while the dress is okay, the boots are men's attire, which makes the wearer displeasing to the Lord. Thank goodness I don't live in Scotland, where my wardrobe would probably include a kilt, and I'd be in trouble.

Forbidden outfits for women (license from Shutterstock.com)

Later in the same chapter of Deuteronomy (Chapter 22), verses 28-29, we find that if a man rapes a virgin woman and it is found out, then he is obligated to pay her father fifty pieces of silver, and then he must marry her. Moreover, he is not permitted to divorce her for as long as he lives.

Remember all those Hollywood war movies where a couple gets married just as the man is about to ship off to war? That is giving a horrible example to the people watching the film, because if you're intent on following the laws of the Bible, then you have other obligations – you have to take a year off from doing any work or military service. Deuteronomy 24:5 specifically says,

⁵When a man hath taken a new wife, he shall not go out to war, neither shall he be charged with any business: but he shall be free at home one year, and shall cheer up his wife which he hath taken.

Photo by Lt. Victor Jorgensen

Imagine what this would do to our armed forces… still, to be righteous in the eyes of God, it's something that should be done. I'm guilty of this one as well – when my wife and I were married, we were just getting started in life and needed every penny of every paycheck. There's no way that I could have taken a year off from work.

Continuing to examine the Old Testament, there is one particular law that would definitely thin the herd of humanity to a huge extent in our world today: Deuteronomy 22:13-21 is very clear that if a couple wed and the woman isn't a virgin, then she must be executed. Can you imagine enforcing such a law today?

I fear that I may have belabored my point, but I could do this forever. There are simply too many Biblical laws to discuss. We are not to ingest any fat (Leviticus 3:17), which pretty much bans us from eating any fast-food at all. And speaking of fast-food, we can't eat bacon on a cheeseburger that we get from the drive-thru, because Leviticus 11:7 says that pork products are unclean.

Which reminds me – a prominent American fast-food chain took a hard stand against homosexuality a while back, and of course one of the main reasons why was Leviticus 18:22 that we looked at before:

22Thou shalt not lie with mankind, as with womankind: it is abomination.

The only problem is that the fast-food chain sells breakfast meals that contain bacon and sausage, which is forbidden just a few chapters earlier in Leviticus.

In any case, you don't need to be telling any dirty jokes to your friends – Ephesians 5:4 warns us against obscenity, foolish talk, or coarse joking. And if a minister tells you to do something, you'd better hop right to it, otherwise you are to be put to death, as prescribed in Deuteronomy 17:12.

It goes on and on. My point – that I've probably had a little too much fun with – is that some people love to pull a single verse out of a book like Leviticus and use it to the beliefs or behavior of others, yet they completely ignore all of the other laws laid down within a few verses of it.

While it is very unfortunate, people love to throw the Old Testament law in the face of anyone with an interest in the supernatural, while ignoring all of the other Old Testament directives.

So when someone accuses me of flying in the face of God with my interest in the supernatural, I just say, "I guess you're probably right... but wait... are those reading glasses in your pocket? You're not planning on going to church, are you?"

Before moving on, though, I have to mention one of my other favorite verses; if two guys are fighting, and the wife of one of them tries to help out her husband by grabbing the other fellow's private parts, then her hand must be cut off. Don't take my word for it – you'll find the law right there in Deuteronomy 25:11-12.

In all seriousness, however, I want to say that I didn't include all this information in this section to make fun of how absurd some of the Old Testament laws are in our world today... although to a large extent, they actually are. Some are downright offensive, such as selling your daughter into slavery (Exodus 21:7), but they were given to a different people at a different time at a time and culture when they somehow made more sense. Trust me, they are no more strange than rules of the Old West might seem to us today.

Many of these Scriptures, however, are used by people to rule on ghosts and the supernatural. Those who do employ them should simply be aware that there are many other scriptures that deserve just as much consideration.

And in that case, the person using the Bible to criticize ghosts and the supernatural would do well to read Matthew 7...

³And why beholdest thou the mote that is in thy brother's eye, but considerest not the beam that is in thine own eye?

⁴Or how wilt thou say to thy brother, Let me pull out the mote out of thine eye; and, behold, a beam is in thine own eye?

⁵Thou hypocrite, first cast out the beam out of thine own eye; and then shalt thou see clearly to cast out the mote out of thy brother's eye.

So basically, I guess you shouldn't criticize someone who has a speck of sawdust in their eye, when you've got a 2x4 in your own. Or to put that more in context, someone really can't criticize your interest in the supernatural while they are wearing a wool/linen blend sweater.

Section 4: How does the Bible Talk About Ghosts?

The last chapter provides a little background about how people use, and misuse, the Word of God and the laws therein. Now let's get into the specifics about the Bible and Ghosts.

You have to be very careful about playing the name game. In his classic work *Romeo and Juliet*, Act II, Scene I, Shakespeare penned the familiar phrase, *What's in a name? That which we call a rose by any other name would smell as sweet.* Case in point, different translations of the Bible use different names for ghosts, spirits, etc., and in fact, those same names may refer to the same thing, or to many different things within a single translation.

There always has been – and probably will be – great debate about scriptures in the Bible describing ghosts. One reason for this is that people must go to great extremes to make any belief fit within their own theology, much like pounding a square peg into a round hole.

A good example is the explanation for the sun in early civilizations. Since the concept of planets and stars was incomprehensible at that time, people rationalized an explanation that was comfortable and acceptable within their particular understanding of the world in their day and age.

Take the ancient Greeks, for example. As the Greek culture developed, they concluded that the giant light that rose every morning, traveled across the sky, and then disappeared every evening could only be a god driving his fiery chariot across the sky. He was given the name Helios, and the shining steeds that pulled his chariot were Pyrios, Aeos, Aethon and Phlegon. What seems like a ridiculous explanation to us today, in fact, made perfect sense to the Greeks.

The Romans had a similar thought about the sun – their chariot-driver was named Sol Invictus. And just like in those old cultures, today people feel the need to bend explanations to fit their world. If someone doesn't believe in ghosts, then it's imperative that he find was in the Bible to discount the whole idea, or write it off as evil, demonic, or wrong.

There's an old saying that describes this way of thinking perfectly: "If all you've got is a hammer, then the entire world looks like a nail." In other words, you adapt your view of everything to fit what limitations you have at hand... like many try to adapt the Bible to fit their beliefs.

But getting back to Shakespeare's rose, what does the Bible use the name of "ghost" to represent?

Giving up the Ghost

Certainly the Bible uses the term "ghost" to mean the human spirit or soul. Throughout the scriptures, the term "give up the ghost" is used to mean that the physical body has died, but the sprit, soul or the "ghost," moves on. Here are just a few examples from the book of Genesis...

Genesis 25:8: *Then Abraham gave up the ghost, and died in a good old age, an old man, and full of years; and was gathered to his people.*

Genesis 25:17: *And these are the years of the life of Ishmael, an hundred and thirty and seven years: and he gave up the ghost and died; and was gathered unto his people.*

Genesis 35:29: *And Isaac gave up the ghost, and died, and was gathered unto his people, being old and full of days: and his sons Esau and Jacob buried him.*

Genesis 49:33: *And when Jacob had made an end of commanding his sons, he gathered up his feet into the bed, and yielded up the ghost, and was gathered unto his people.*

The Soul Leaving the Body by Luigi Schiavonetti, c. 1810

Notice that in the previous verses, not only do they say that the person dies, but he gives up the ghost, and then was "gathered unto his people." If you read through modern translations of the Bible, the consensus is that giving up the ghost indicates death of the body, and the soul leaving it; gathering unto his people is translated to joining his relatives and loved ones that have passed on.

"Giving up the ghost" is not a term that is limited to the first book of the Bible, however. The references continue throughout, and here are a few more to look at:

Job 3:11: *Why died I not from the womb? Why did I not give up the ghost when I came out of the belly?*

Job 14:10: *But man dieth, and wasteth away: yea, man giveth up the ghost, and where is he?*

Lamentations 1:19: *I called for my lovers, but they deceived me: my priests and mine elders gave up the ghost in the city, while they sought their meat to relieve their souls.*

Matthew 27:50: *Jesus, when he had cried again with a loud voice, yielded up the ghost.*

Mark 15:37: *And Jesus cried with a loud voice, and gave up the ghost.*

Mark 15:39: *And when the centurion, which stood over against him, saw that he so cried out, and gave up the ghost, he said, Truly this man was the Son of God.*

Luke 23:46: *And when Jesus had cried with a loud voice, he said, Father, into thy hands I commend my spirit: and having said thus, he gave up the ghost.*

John 19:30: *When Jesus therefore had received the vinegar, he said, It is finished: and he bowed his head, and gave up the ghost.*

Acts 5:5: *And Ananias hearing these words fell down, and gave up the ghost: and great fear came on all them that heard these things.*

Acts 5:10: *Then fell she down straightway at his feet, and yielded up the ghost: and the young men came in, and found her dead, and, carrying her forth, buried her by her husband.*

Acts 12:23: *And immediately the angel of the Lord smote him, because he gave not God the glory: and he was eaten of worms, and gave up the ghost.*

All in all, the term "giving up the ghost" is prevalent throughout the Bible, and is always used to mean that the soul, spirit, or ghost (call it what you will) left the body.

Familiar Spirits

What are familiar spirits? The Bible certainly mentions them a lot, as in someone having a "familiar spirit"... and it's always used in a very negative term. Here are just a few examples of verses containing that phrase:

Deuteronomy 18:10-12: *There shall not be found among you any one that maketh his son or his daughter to pass through the fire, or that useth divination, or an observer of times, or an enchanter, or a witch. Or a charmer, or a consulter with familiar spirits, or a wizard, or a necromancer. For all that do these things are an abomination unto the Lord: and because of these abominations the Lord thy God doth drive them out from before thee.*

2 Kings 21:6: *And he made his son pass through the fire, and observed times, and used enchantments, and* *dealt with familiar spirits and wizards: he wrought much wickedness in the sight of the Lord, to provoke him to anger.*

2 Chronicles 33:6: *And he caused his children to pass through the fire in the valley of the son of Hinnom: also he observed times, and used enchantments, and used witchcraft, and dealt with a familiar spirit, and with wizards: he wrought much evil in the sight of the LORD, to provoke him to anger.*

Leviticus 19:31: *Regard not them that have familiar spirits, neither seek after wizards, to be defiled by them: I am the Lord your God.*

Leviticus 20:6: *And the soul that turneth after such as have familiar spirits, and after wizards, to go a whoring after them, I will even set my face against that soul, and will cut him off from among his people.*

Isaiah 8:19: *And when they shall say unto you, Seek unto them that have familiar spirits, and unto wizards that peep, and that mutter: should not a people seek unto their God? for the living to the dead?*

Isaiah 29:4: *And thou shalt be brought down, and shalt speak out of the ground, and thy speech shall be low out of the dust, and thy voice shall be, as of one that hath a familiar spirit, out of the ground, and thy speech shall whisper out of the dust.*

So what are these "familiar spirits"? Since the term is bantered around so much in the scripture, one would think that there would be a clear-cut definition. Unlike the phrase "give up the ghost," though, that's not the case.

Some scholars go with the classic definition from witchcraft. A "familiar spirit" is sometimes called a "familiar," which is derived from the Middle English term that means "related to family." This is an animal spirit of some type that enables its owner to work feats of the supernatural. Many assume that such a spirit is a demon, as you will find with witches and their cliché black cats, owls, mice, etc. from modern literature.

Woodcutting showing the cliché "familiar spirits"

Other people trace the word "familiar" back to the Latin familiaris, meaning a "household servant." Those folks say that it indicates a spirit that is tied to a particular person, and it somehow that aids him or her in contacting the dead, working magic, or other feats of the supernatural.

Yet another explanation is that the term "familiar spirits" refers to evil spirits that are familiar with a person's ancestral past. These evil spirits use their

47

familiarity to bring the same curses and problems that a person's parents or ancestors encountered during their lives. Familiar spirits are therefore carriers of generational curses, passing the same afflictions from one generation to another.

In *Bamford's Bible Dictionary*, you will see that the term "familiar spirits" applies to the general practice of communicating with the spirits of the dead. In other words, a human is placing themselves in a position to be "familiar" with spirits.

On the other hand, *Easton's Bible Dictionary* says that the practice of having familiar spirits involved sorcerers, mediums or necromancers, who had the ability to call up the dead to answer questions. These individuals were said to have a "familiar spirit" of another dead person. Its moniker comes from the familiarity that it has with a living person. For example, a woman that Paul encountered in Macedonia had a familiar spirit which gave her powers of divination.

Not to belabor the point, there are people that say that the person in question was "familiar" with the spirit, in that he or she was actually trying to contact it. In the world of ghost-hunting today, that might include trying to capture a voice on EVP, a spirit in a photograph, or a spike on an EMF meter.

So which one of these definitions of "familiar spirit" is correct? Who knows – flip a coin, draw straws, but there is one thing that is very curious. If the concept of familiar spirits is so important to the text of the Bible, why isn't it clearly defined for the reader? That will always puzzle me, because it leaves the interpretation open to everyone's particular whims and individual beliefs.

Unclean Spirits

As we continue to look for spirits in the Bible, there is another type worth mentioning. It seems that there are many mentions of "unclean spirits" in the Bible, which seems to differentiate them from "familiar spirits" or the type of spirit that is "given up," the latter two, of course, we've already discussed. Here are some sample verses from the King James Version of the Bible regarding unclean spirits:

Mark 3:11: *And unclean spirits, when they saw him, fell down before him, and cried, saying, Thou art the Son of God.*

Mark 5:2-4: *And when he was come out of the ship, immediately there met him out of the tombs a man with an unclean spirit, who had his dwelling among the tombs; and no man could bind him, no, not with chains: because that he had been often bound with fetters and chains, and the chains had been plucked asunder by him, and the fetters broken in pieces: neither could any man tame him.*

Mark 6:7: *And he called unto him the twelve, and began to send them forth by two and two; and gave them power over unclean spirits;*

Luke 4:36: *And they were all amazed, and spake among themselves, saying, What a word is this! for with authority and power he commandeth the unclean spirits, and they come out.*

Luke 6:18: *And they that were vexed with unclean spirits: and they were healed.*

Acts 8:7: *For unclean spirits, crying with loud voice, came out of many that were possessed with them: and many taken with palsies, and that were lame, were healed.*

49

Revelation 16:13: *And I saw three unclean spirits like frogs come out of the mouth of the dragon, and out of the mouth of the beast, and out of the mouth of the false prophet.*

In the Bible, unclean spirits were blamed for sickness, physical afflictions, mental illness, demonic possession, and any number of negative things.

Jesus cast out unclean spirits, as his disciples were given the power to do that as well. One of the most well-known stories about Christ dealing with unclean spirits comes from the book of Mark, Chapter 5:

[1]And they came over unto the other side of the sea, into the country of the Gadarenes.

[2]And when he was come out of the ship, immediately there met him out of the tombs a man with an unclean spirit,

[3]Who had his dwelling among the tombs; and no man could bind him, no, not with chains:

[4]Because that he had been often bound with fetters and chains, and the chains had been plucked asunder by him, and the fetters broken in pieces: neither could any man tame him.

[5]And always, night and day, he was in the mountains, and in the tombs, crying, and cutting himself with stones.

[6]But when he saw Jesus afar off, he ran and worshipped him,

[7]And cried with a loud voice, and said, What have I to do with thee, Jesus, thou Son of the most high God? I adjure thee by God, that thou torment me not.

⁸*For he said unto him, Come out of the man, thou unclean spirit.*

⁹*And he asked him, What is thy name? And he answered, saying, My name is Legion: for we are many.*

¹⁰*And he besought him much that he would not send them away out of the country.*

¹¹*Now there was there nigh unto the mountains a great herd of swine feeding.*

¹²*And all the devils besought him, saying, Send us into the swine, that we may enter into them.*

¹³*And forthwith Jesus gave them leave. And the unclean spirits went out, and entered into the swine: and the herd ran violently down a steep place into the sea, (they were about two thousand;) and were choked in the sea.*

¹⁴*And they that fed the swine fled, and told it in the city, and in the country. And they went out to see what it was that was done.*

¹⁵*And they come to Jesus, and see him that was possessed with the devil, and had the legion, sitting, and clothed, and in his right mind: and they were afraid.*

¹⁶*And they that saw it told them how it befell to him that was possessed with the devil, and also concerning the swine.*

¹⁷*And they began to pray him to depart out of their coasts.*

¹⁸*And when he was come into the ship, he that had been possessed with the devil prayed him that he might be with him.*

¹⁹*Howbeit Jesus suffered him not, but saith unto him, Go home to thy friends, and tell them how great things the*

51

Lord hath done for thee, and hath had compassion on thee.

Woodcutting of Jesus casting out unclean spirits

From Mark 5:1-19, it is clear that these "unclean spirits" were demons. Not only did they recognize Jesus, but they begged him to let them possess a herd of swine when he cast them out of the man… and the beasts ran into the sea and drowned.

The Biblical references to unclean spirits seem to always point to demons, whether they be causing illness, madness, or just a negative disposition in the person that they happened to be possessing. This is different from the references of "giving up the ghost" – or "giving up the spirit" in some translations, and also from "familiar spirits."

The references to ghosts or spirits in the Bible seem to mean different things, so perhaps it's worth looking at the various entities that exist in our world, even though some people might refer to it as "supernatural."

Angels vs. Demons vs. Ghosts

This book is about ghosts, the spirits or souls of humans that are our very essence. There are, however, other supernatural beings that share this world with us.

There are a host of other beings that are part of our Earthly lives that we minimalize, if not downright ignore. They are the beings beyond our "natural" world, which would fall into the class of "beyond the natural," or supernatural... "beyond the normal," or paranormal. These are angels and demons. In this chapter, we're going to examine what each of them are, and therefore the differences between them.

Angels

The Bible tells us that the angels were witnesses when God created the Earth, so apparently they were created long before the big event happened.

When Job was questioning God about the terrible things that had happened to him, God answered:

[4]Where wast thou when I laid the foundations of the earth? declare, if thou hast understanding.

[5]Who hath laid the measures thereof, if thou knowest? or who hath stretched the line upon it?

[6]Whereupon are the foundations thereof fastened? or who laid the corner stone thereof;

⁷When the morning stars sang together, and all the sons of God shouted for joy?

God was basically saying, "You think that you have all of the answers, but where were you when I created the Earth?" In other words – "I made everything in the world, so how dare you question Me?"

In verse 7, though, He is talking specifically about the angels; they were there, and rejoiced when they saw the Earth being created. The angels were in existence long before man.

Other parts of the Scripture show that the angels were created to do God's will. In fact, the word "angel" actually means "messenger" or "agent." Psalm 103:20 says,

²⁰Bless the LORD, ye his angels, that excel in strength, that do his commandments, hearkening unto the voice of his word.

Angels also are charged by God with taking care of humans, and in fact, they probably do much more than we will ever know in that regard. Psalm 91:11 says,

¹¹For he shall give his angels charge over thee, to keep thee in all thy ways.

Angels show up throughout the scripture; they delivered a message to Lot in the city of Sodom before its destruction, an angel closed the mouths of the lions when Daniel was thrown into their den to be executed, and they continue to do God's bidding here on Earth.

In fact, angels are apparently moving around in our

world undetected, because the Bible cautions us in Hebrews 13:2,

²*Be not forgetful to entertain strangers: for thereby some have entertained angels unawares.*

In other words, we encounter angels all the time, going about on their duties, but we just don't recognize them as such. It amazes me to stop and think that I've probably encountered any number of angles in the course of the average day, but just assume that they were human beings like me.

An Angel protecting Daniel in the lions' den

Demons

Satan, Lucifer, Beelzebub, or as we call him, the Devil, was once the perfect angel – beautiful, moral, and

55

sinless. He had free access to the presence of God, and was one of His favorites (all described in Ezekiel 28:11-19, where Satan is described as the "King of Tyre").

The Bible itself doesn't tell a lot about Satan's fall from grace, but 1 Timothy 3:6 indicates that his demise came from pride. According to legend, Satan began to believe that he was as great as God Himself, and therefore led a rebellion of fallen angels against the Almighty and the angels loyal to him.

Woodcutting depicting the artist's view of a demon

After a great battle, the fallen angels – or demons, as they would come to be called – were defeated and faced an eternal damnation in the pit of Hell. Until that banishment comes, however, demons are free to roam the

Earth doing Satan's bidding, just as the angels do on behalf of God.

Instead of being messengers or gentle agents, the demons seek to be tricksters and deceivers of humans, entrapping them into the corrupt ways of sin, and causing people a world of hurt and misery. As mentioned earlier in the chapter, demons are referred to as "unclean spirits" throughout the Bible.

Lucifer Versus The Lord by Mihaly Zichy, c. 1902

57

The demons of our world are not necessarily hideous creatures, though, because 2 Corinthians 11:14 tells us that for the purpose of deceiving the innocent, *Satan himself is transformed into an angel of light.* This appearance of piety would be the perfect disguise for deceiving humans, and is one that I am sure he has used quite often and with great effect.

Since angels and demons were all created as the same type of beings, their powers and abilities must be identically strong – it's just that the former is good, and the latter is certainly evil. In movies like *The Exorcist* and *The Omen* Hollywood mistakenly portrays Satan and his demons as being all-powerful. It is instead clear that all things, whether they be angels, demons, or Satan himself, must answer to God, the creator of all. Isaiah 45 says:

> *⁶That they may know from the rising of the sun, and from the west, that there is none beside me. I am the* LORD, *and there is none else.*
>
> *⁷I form the light, and create darkness: I make peace, and create evil: I the* LORD *do all these things.*
>
> *⁸Drop down, ye heavens, from above, and let the skies pour down righteousness: let the earth open, and let them bring forth salvation, and let righteousness spring up together; I the* LORD *have created it.*

So, at the end of the day, God is the creator of all things in our world, and the next. More than that, though, he is in charge of all things in Heaven and on Earth: humans, spirits, angels, demons, or anything else that you can name are subject to him. There is no creature of any form that is not subject to God. Deuteronomy 4:39 says,

Know therefore this day, and consider it in thine heart, that the LORD he is God in heaven above, and upon the earth beneath: there is none else.

...and that gives me great comfort.

Section 5: Case Studies from the Scriptures

The Light at the Top of the Mountain

One topic of debate, when it comes to ghosts, breaks down into a couple of very simple questions: Can the dead return to Earth in a recognizable form? And if so, do they have the ability to interact with the people here?

Actually, the Bible has several instances of this occurring, and probably one of the most interesting, yet controversial is described the Book of Matthew, where the story is told of Moses and Elijah coming back for a brief visit during the event that is commonly known as the "transfiguration."

This story is so fascinating to me that it is the namesake for this book. With that said, let's take a look at the transfiguration, the light at the top of the mountain, which is described in the Book of Matthew, Chapter 17:

[1]*And after six days Jesus taketh Peter, James, and John his brother, and bringeth them up into an high*

mountain apart,

²And was transfigured before them, and his face did shine as the sun, and his raiment was white as the light,

³And, behold, there appeared unto them Moses and Elias talking with him.

⁴Then answered Peter, and said unto Jesus, Lord, it is good for us to be here. If thou wilt, let us make here three tabernacles, one for thee, and one for Moses, and one for Elias.

⁵While he yet spake, behold, a bright cloud overshadowed them, and behold a voice out of the cloud, which said, This is my beloved Son, in whom I am well pleased; hear ye him.

⁶And when the disciples heard it, they fell on their face, and were sore afraid.

⁷And Jesus came and touched them, and said, Arise, and be not afraid.

⁸And when they had lifted up their eyes, they saw no man, save Jesus only.

This is a very interesting passage of scripture; a lot of things happen in the course of those eight short verses. First, Jesus takes three of his disciples to the top of a mountain. Once they get there, he begins to shine brilliantly with what most interpret to be the very power and divinity of God. Suddenly, the disciples see that Moses and Elias (Elijah) have shown up, and are talking to Jesus. It is such a real experience that Peter offers to build a shelter for each of the three men. At that point, a cloud appears in the sky and God's voice boomed out, alarming the disciples enough that they fell to the ground and hid their eyes. Jesus tells them not to be afraid, and when they look up, Moses, Elijah and the cloud have all disappeared.

The Transfiguration by Carl Heinrich Bloch, c. 1872

We know for a fact that Moses died – the Bible clearly states that fact in Deuteronomy 34:5-6, and furthermore he was buried by God himself. Although there might have been some funny business associated with it – Jude 1:9 says:

⁹Yet Michael the archangel, when contending with the devil he disputed about the body of Moses, durst not bring against him a railing accusation, but said, The Lord rebuke thee.

One has to wonder what Michael and the devil were arguing about concerning Moses' body.

Clearly, however, Moses lived and died, and then came back to Earth on the top of the mountain.

On the other hand, Elijah technically never really died; he was taken directly up to heaven by a whirlwind. Elijah was walking with his understudy Elisha, and 2 Kings 2 describes what happens:

[11]*And it came to pass, as they still went on, and talked, that, behold, there appeared a chariot of fire, and horses of fire, and parted them both asunder; and Elijah went up by a whirlwind into heaven.*

[12]*And Elisha saw it, and he cried, My father, my father, the chariot of Israel, and the horsemen thereof. And he saw him no more: and he took hold of his own clothes, and rent them in two pieces.*

Still, Elijah had crossed the boundary between this world and the next, even though he did so without actually dying, he did manage to come back to the mountaintop.

The Bible is very clear that both Moses and Elijah did return; consider the definitive statement in the three gospel accounts of the transfiguration:

Matthew 17:3: *And, behold, there appeared unto them Moses and Elias talking with him.*

Mark 9:4: *And there appeared unto them Elias with Moses; and they were talking with Jesus.*

Luke 9:30: *And, behold, there talked with him two men, which were Moses and Elias.*

The entire passage in Matthew was presented at the first of this chapter, and please feel free to read the accounts of Mark and Luke in full context. What seems to be very clear is that Moses and Elijah both showed up on the top of the mountain that day – the Bible doesn't call them visions, or dreams, or anything else imaginary. They were so definitively there that Jesus was actually conversing with them, all of which was witnessed by the disciples.

The Transfiguration by Raphael, c. 1520

It's interesting that when the disciples first saw Jesus after the resurrection they thought that he was a ghost, but here, they didn't question the same thing about the two prophets. Another odd aspect of the event is that the disciples apparently knew who both Moses and Elijah were right away, even though both men had been dead hundreds of years before. If Grover Cleveland and Richard Nixon both appeared before me, I might recognize Nixon, but I'd have no idea who Cleveland was, even though he'd been President of the United States less than 100 years before I was born.

The disciples' recognition of the two men adds to the mystery of the event, and may imply some Divine inspiration bestowed on them.

A final note on this story is that Jesus was talking with Moses and Elijah – clearly it is possible to communicate with those who have died, and the Lord chose to show this fact to Peter, James and John.

All that aside, however, it is more than clear that Moses and Elijah were standing there on the top of the mountain with Jesus. Call them what you want, but if I saw Cleveland and Nixon standing in my back yard, I'd call them ghosts.

A Spirit from the Book of Job

In the Old Testament Book of Job, the story is told of a deeply religious and righteous man of that name. He loves his family so much that he regularly offers burnt offerings to God to forgive their sins as well as his.

Meanwhile, in the world beyond our own, Satan showed up to call on God. As the Scripture says in Job 2:

¹Again there was a day when the sons of God came to present themselves before the Lord, and Satan came also among them to present himself before the Lord.
²And the Lord said unto Satan, From whence comest thou? And Satan answered the Lord, and said, From going to and fro in the earth, and from walking up and

down in it.

³And the Lord said unto Satan, Hast thou considered my servant Job, that there is none like him in the earth, a perfect and an upright man, one that feareth God, and escheweth evil? and still he holdeth fast his integrity, although thou movedst me against him, to destroy him without cause.

⁴And Satan answered the Lord, and said, Skin for skin, yea, all that a man hath will he give for his life.

⁵But put forth thine hand now, and touch his bone and his flesh, and he will curse thee to thy face.

⁶And the Lord said unto Satan, Behold, he is in thine hand; but save his life.

Basically, God tells Satan, "Hey, check out my homeboy Job – quite a fellow, eh?"

Satan replies, "Sure, it's easy for him to praise you with everything that you've give him – but reach out your hand and strike him down, and I'll bet that he's cursing you before you know it."

Having been challenged, God tells Satan, "Okay, he's yours. Do your worst and we'll see if he doesn't hold up to whatever you can dish out." Before setting him loose on Job, however, God gives him one restriction: "You cannot take his life."

To make a long story short, Satan gives it his best shot. He strips Job of pretty much everything – the Sabeans, basically marauders, stole his 500 yoke of oxen and 500 donkeys. They also killed all of his servants tending the cattle, leaving only one to return and tell Job the bad news.

As Job was digesting that news, another servant ran

up and told him that "the fire of God" came down from the sky and burned up not only 7,001 sheep, but the shepherds tending them, leaving only one who could report back to Job.

Next a servant approached and told Job that his 3,000 camels had been stolen by a band of thieves that were called the Chaldeans. Of course, they killed all of the camel-tenders with their swords, leaving only one to come and tell Job.

Job and his Friends by Ilya Repin, c. 1869

Finally, a house servant of Job's eldest son approaches. He says that all ten of Job's children were dining in the home of the oldest brother when a violent wind came and collapsed the house on top of them, killing everyone inside – his kids as well as all of the house servants. Except, as you might guess, for the one servant that was left to come and give Job the tragic news.

In a day, all of Job's possessions and children were taken from him – yet he did not curse God. The rest of the book is concerned with further things that happen to Job, and his interaction not only with God, but with four of his friends: Eliphaz the Temanite, Bildad the Shuhite, Zophar the Naamathite, and Elihu the Buzite.

The interesting thing about the Book of Job, for the purposes of our discussion, is that when Eliphaz is talking to Job, he tells him about an encounter with a ghost. It is in Chapter 4:

^{12}*Now a thing was secretly brought to me, and mine ear received a little thereof.*

^{13}*In thoughts from the visions of the night, when deep sleep falleth on men,*

^{14}*Fear came upon me, and trembling, which made all my bones to shake.*

^{15}*Then a spirit passed before my face; the hair of my flesh stood up:*

^{16}*It stood still, but I could not discern the form thereof: an image was before mine eyes, there was silence, and I heard a voice, saying,*

^{17}*Shall mortal man be more just than God? shall a man be more pure than his maker?*

Clearly the spirit was there to deliver a message to Eliphaz, but the fascinating thing is his description of the encounter – the spirit passed in front of his face, and then the "hair of his flesh" stood up, which is a common experience with people who have had an experience with a ghost. It's something that is characterized all the time:

"The hair on my arms and the back of my neck stood up!"

Eliphaz goes on to say that he couldn't make out the exact form of the spirit as it stood before him, but there was definitely a figure there.

I have almost the exact same story from an investigation of the Jefferson Hotel in the historic city of Jefferson, Texas, where a couple woke up in the middle of the night to see the spirit-form of a young lady standing at the foot of the bed – and here a near-identical story is in the Bible.

The Chasm Between Heaven and Hell

I'm including this even though it doesn't directly indicate that there is a passage that is possible between the afterlife and Earth. In this case, it's less about what is said, and more about what isn't. Before going too far down that road, however, consider Luke 16:19-31…

[19]*There was a certain rich man, which was clothed in purple and fine linen, and fared sumptuously every day:*

[20]*And there was a certain beggar named Lazarus, which was laid at his gate, full of sores,*

[21]*And desiring to be fed with the crumbs which fell from the rich man's table: moreover the dogs came and licked his sores.*

[22]*And it came to pass, that the beggar died, and was carried by the angels into Abraham's bosom: the rich man also died, and was buried;*

[23]*And in hell he lift up his eyes, being in torments, and seeth Abraham afar off, and Lazarus in his bosom.*

[24]*And he cried and said, Father Abraham, have mercy on me, and send Lazarus, that he may dip the tip of his*

finger in water, and cool my tongue; for I am tormented in this flame.

[25] But Abraham said, Son, remember that thou in thy lifetime receivedst thy good things, and likewise Lazarus evil things: but now he is comforted, and thou art tormented.

[26] And beside all this, between us and you there is a great gulf fixed: so that they which would pass from hence to you cannot; neither can they pass to us, that would come from thence.

[27] Then he said, I pray thee therefore, father, that thou wouldest send him to my father's house:

[28] For I have five brethren; that he may testify unto them, lest they also come into this place of torment.

[29] Abraham saith unto him, They have Moses and the prophets; let them hear them.

[30] And he said, Nay, father Abraham: but if one went unto them from the dead, they will repent.

[31] And he said unto him, If they hear not Moses and the prophets, neither will they be persuaded, though one rose from the dead.

As I pointed out a moment ago, the interesting thing is not what is said, but instead what isn't. Looking back at the scripture, a rich man living the life of luxury saw a beggar named Lazarus, but did nothing to help him.

Lazarus died and went to heaven, while the rich man died and went to hell. As the rich man was roasting in the fires of Hades, he begged Abraham in Heaven to allow Lazarus to come down, dip his finger and water, and let it drip on his tongue.

Abraham answered quickly – not possible, can't do it,

no way, and the reason was that a "great gulf" had been put in between heaven and hell, and there was no way to move between the two places.

The rich man then said, "Okay, but I have five brothers back on Earth. Can you send Lazarus to warn them not to live like I did, so that they won't end up here?"

Woodcutting of Abraham and Lazarus

Here's the part that's most interesting to me... Abraham didn't say "Hey, just like the great gulf between heaven and hell, we can't go back to Earth either!" No, he never denied the possibility of the trip back. Instead, he simply said, "Hey, Moses and the prophets are over there, and if your brothers won't listen to them, they're certainly not going to listen to Lazarus."

While Abraham throws up a huge roadblock between traveling from Heaven to Hell in this passage, he leaves the road open between Heaven and Earth.

So Great a Cloud of Witnesses

I remember several years ago when I was younger – and thinner – than I am today, and I ran in the annual Thanksgiving Day Turkey Trot in Dallas, Texas. I'd trained for the eight-mile run all summer long, and was really looking forward to doing it. Thanksgiving Day came, and early that morning I drove downtown, pinned the paper competition number that they gave me onto my tee shirt, and started running when the starter pistol was fired. I wasn't the fastest one there, but I steadily marked off mile after mile. About halfway through it started to sleet, something that I wasn't prepared for. Ice was forming on the paper number on my chest, I started worrying about slipping on the pavement, and the frigid air was permeating my body all the way through to my bones.

By the last mile I was freezing, and having to constantly worry about my footing was exhausting me. As I approached the finish line, however, I saw a huge crowd that was cheering the runners on as they completed the race. They were huddled under umbrellas and wrapped up in heavy coats, but they were clapping and yelling at the top of their lungs as each runner went by. It charged me up and inspired me to the point where I got an incredible burst of energy and crossed the finish line with my head held high – no problem at all.

Because of that experience, I completely understand Hebrews 12:1, which says:

¹Wherefore seeing we also are compassed about with so great a cloud of witnesses, let us lay aside every weight, and the sin which doth so easily beset us, and let us run with patience the race that is set before us.

It's like that verse was written specifically about me running the race on that Thanksgiving Day. In the context of the chapter and Book of Hebrews, everyone pretty much agrees that the "witnesses" refers to the people who have died and gone on before us.

Chapter 12, Verse 1, is a continuation of Hebrews Chapter 11, whose Verse 1 states,

¹Now faith is the substance of things hoped for, the evidence of things not seen.

Chapter 11 goes on to list a number of people in the Bible who acted on faith, including Abel, Enoch, Noah, Sara, Abraham, Isaac, Jacob, Joseph, Moses, Rahab, David, and Samuel. This is just a few of the people, though, because Verse 32 in that chapter goes on to say that there isn't enough time to tell about everyone:

³²And what shall I more say? for the time would fail me to tell of Gedeon, and of Barak, and of Samson, and of Jephthae; of David also, and Samuel, and of the prophets.

Chapter 12 continues this thought, describing all of these people, the dead, as a "cloud of witnesses" that surround us – those listed, and those countless more that there weren't time to talk about. But by using the analogy of running a race, this passage indicates that those who

74

have gone on before us are watching us, and are supporters of our efforts – the dead are not removed from our experiences here on Earth as many might believe.

The Lord Takes a Watery Stroll

Talk about a big day – Jesus had just performed one of his many miracles, feeding a throng of people with a mere five loaves of bread and two fish. Afterwards, he performed another miracle, one of his most famous: walking on water. It's one that has been chronicled through the ages: Aerosmith named a song after it, Lynyrd Skynyrd memorialized it with their lyrics, "Jesus walked on water – I know that it's true," and it's become a staple of our daily conversation for describing someone who is good: "That fellow walks on water." While Luke completely ignored the whole event, and John minimalized it by saying that Jesus got into the boat more or less when it got back to shore, Matthew and Mark both described something that only Jesus could have accomplished: walking across the turbulent waters in the middle of a sea. Of course, this is no small feat. I can't begin to imagine why it wasn't covered by half of the gospels, but that's not our current concern. What's much more interesting is what happened in Matthew and Mark when Jesus walked across the water.

To set the stage, the miracle of feeding the multitudes had just occurred, and Jesus had gone up onto a mountain to pray. His disciples got into a boat and went out onto a lake, but the story picks up in Matthew 14:

[22]And straightway Jesus constrained his disciples to get into a ship, and to go before him unto the other side,

while he sent the multitudes away.

²³And when he had sent the multitudes away, he went up into a mountain apart to pray: and when the evening was come, he was there alone.

²⁴But the ship was now in the midst of the sea, tossed with waves: for the wind was contrary.

²⁵And in the fourth watch of the night Jesus went unto them, walking on the sea.

²⁶And when the disciples saw him walking on the sea, they were troubled, saying, It is a spirit; and they cried out for fear.

²⁷But straightway Jesus spake unto them, saying, Be of good cheer; it is I; be not afraid.

²⁸And Peter answered him and said, Lord, if it be thou, bid me come unto thee on the water.

²⁹And he said, Come. And when Peter was come down out of the ship, he walked on the water, to go to Jesus.

³⁰But when he saw the wind boisterous, he was afraid; and beginning to sink, he cried, saying, Lord, save me.

³¹And immediately Jesus stretched forth his hand, and caught him, and said unto him, O thou of little faith, wherefore didst thou doubt?

³²And when they were come into the ship, the wind ceased.

³³Then they that were in the ship came and worshipped him, saying, Of a truth thou art the Son of God.

³⁴And when they were gone over, they came into the land of Gennesaret.

The most interesting thing – other than Jesus having the power to walk on the water, of course – is in verses 26 and 27. When the disciples see him crossing the sea they assume that he is a ghost coming toward them, and they directly say as much. Jesus immediately answers them and basically, says something like, "Hey, don't worry – it's me! Don't panic!"

Jesus Walking on the Waters by Julius Klever, c. 1901

Mark, in his own Gospel, tells the same story in Chapter 6:

⁴⁹But when they saw him walking upon the sea, they supposed it had been a spirit, and cried out:
⁵⁰For they all saw him, and were troubled. And immediately he talked with them, and saith unto them, Be of good cheer: it is I; be not afraid.

⁵¹And he went up unto them into the ship; and the wind ceased: and they were sore amazed in themselves beyond measure, and wondered.

⁵²For they considered not the miracle of the loaves: for their heart was hardened.

John doesn't write about them thinking that Jesus is a ghost, but in Chapter 6 as he recounts the story he does say that they were afraid:

¹⁹So when they had rowed about five and twenty or thirty furlongs, they see Jesus walking on the sea, and drawing nigh unto the ship: and they were afraid.

²⁰But he saith unto them, It is I; be not afraid.

²¹Then they willingly received him into the ship: and immediately the ship was at the land whither they went.

This event took place in the early morning hours, while it was certainly still dark – which would have made the image of a figure walking across the water seem frightening to the disciples. Matthew 14, which was previously quoted, says that Jesus went to them in the fourth watch of the night, walking on the sea. In nautical history, on a ship someone is always on duty as the night watch. There are four such shifts, so each night is divided into four parts of three hours each. Since night begins at sunset, which without Daylight Saving Time, can be considered to be around 6 PM. The fourth, or last watch of the night before sunrise, takes place between 3 AM and 6 AM, which is when they would have seen this miracle.

As the Son of God, it's no great mystery that Jesus could walk on the water. The real mystery for us is that when the disciples were frightened out of their minds and said, "It's a ghost!!!" why didn't Jesus answer, "Hey, c'mon, there's no such things as ghosts," or instead, "Ghosts are satanic and evil – don't compare me to such things." No, instead he calmly said the olden-times equivalent of "Chill out dudes, it's only me. Calm down, for cryin' out loud." He didn't get excited about being mistaken for a ghost at all.

"The Witch of Endor" Problem

There is a very interesting story in the Bible about the Witch of Endor, and it is told in 1 Samuel, Chapter 28.

[1]And it came to pass in those days, that the Philistines gathered their armies together for warfare, to fight with Israel. And Achish said unto David, Know thou assuredly, that thou shalt go out with me to battle, thou and thy men.

[2]And David said to Achish, Surely thou shalt know what thy servant can do. And Achish said to David, Therefore will I make thee keeper of mine head for ever.

[3]Now Samuel was dead, and all Israel had lamented him, and buried him in Ramah, even in his own city. And Saul had put away those that had familiar spirits, and the wizards, out of the land.

[4]And the Philistines gathered themselves together, and came and pitched in Shunem: and Saul gathered all Israel together, and they pitched in Gilboa.

[5]And when Saul saw the host of the Philistines, he was afraid, and his heart greatly trembled.

[6]And when Saul enquired of the LORD, the LORD answered him not, neither by dreams, nor by Urim, nor by prophets.

⁷*Then said Saul unto his servants, Seek me a woman that hath a familiar spirit, that I may go to her, and enquire of her. And his servants said to him, Behold, there is a woman that hath a familiar spirit at Endor.*

⁸*And Saul disguised himself, and put on other raiment, and he went, and two men with him, and they came to the woman by night: and he said, I pray thee, divine unto me by the familiar spirit, and bring me him up, whom I shall name unto thee.*

⁹*And the woman said unto him, Behold, thou knowest what Saul hath done, how he hath cut off those that have familiar spirits, and the wizards, out of the land: wherefore then layest thou a snare for my life, to cause me to die?*

¹⁰*And Saul sware to her by the LORD, saying, As the LORD liveth, there shall no punishment happen to thee for this thing.*

¹¹*Then said the woman, Whom shall I bring up unto thee? And he said, Bring me up Samuel.*

¹²*And when the woman saw Samuel, she cried with a loud voice: and the woman spake to Saul, saying, Why hast thou deceived me? for thou art Saul.*

¹³*And the king said unto her, Be not afraid: for what sawest thou? And the woman said unto Saul, I saw gods ascending out of the earth.*

¹⁴*And he said unto her, What form is he of? And she said, An old man cometh up; and he is covered with a mantle. And Saul perceived that it was Samuel, and he stooped with his face to the ground, and bowed himself.*

¹⁵*And Samuel said to Saul, Why hast thou disquieted me, to bring me up? And Saul answered, I am sore distressed; for the Philistines make war against me, and*

God is departed from me, and answereth me no more, neither by prophets, nor by dreams: therefore I have called thee, that thou mayest make known unto me what I shall do.

[16]Then said Samuel, Wherefore then dost thou ask of me, seeing the LORD is departed from thee, and is become thine enemy?

[17]And the LORD hath done to him, as he spake by me: for the LORD hath rent the kingdom out of thine hand, and given it to thy neighbour, even to David:

[18]Because thou obeyedst not the voice of the LORD, nor executedst his fierce wrath upon Amalek, therefore hath the LORD done this thing unto thee this day.

[19]Moreover the LORD will also deliver Israel with thee into the hand of the Philistines: and to morrow shalt thou and thy sons be with me: the LORD also shall deliver the host of Israel into the hand of the Philistines.

[20]Then Saul fell straightway all along on the earth, and was sore afraid, because of the words of Samuel: and there was no strength in him; for he had eaten no bread all the day, nor all the night.

There are several things leading up to the interaction between Saul and the Witch of Endor, and you can read the entire story in First Samuel.

When the Hebrew, God's people, were fleeing Egypt, they ran across a nomadic tribe called the Amalek. Even as they fled, the Amalekites attacked them, killing those who were lagging behind because they were tired and weak – much in the same way that lions on the African plains kill the slowest wildebeests in the herd.

God must be a fan of that old proverb, "Revenge is a

81

dish best served cold," because several hundred years later the prophet Samuel gave King Saul very specific instructions from God. He told Saul to gather his troops and go over to the land of the Amalek and decimate them completely. Not only were the men and women to be killed, but even their children and babies were to be put to the sword. God didn't stop there, however – the Amalekites' animals were to be slaughtered as well. Clearly, God was still very angry with the Amalek.

Being a servant of the Lord, King Saul took his warriors over to the Amalek, where they proceeded to kill every living thing… but somewhere in the course of things, Saul took a detour from his instructions. As they were slaughtering the animals, he must have reasoned that it would be a waste just to let them all die, so he had the best ones spared and taken back home. To make matters worse, though, he took pity on the King of the Amalekites and let him live as well. Everyone else, from newborns to the elderly, was killed by the swords of Saul's warriors.

When Saul and his army returned home, he told Samuel, "I have performed the commandment of the Lord."

Samuel suspected that something was wrong, though, and basically said, "Well, if that is really the case, then what's with all the sheep bleeting and oxen lowing that I keep hearing back there?"

Red-faced, Saul knew that he was caught. "Oh, *those* sheep and oxen. Well, uh, I mean, it wasn't *my* fault – I wanted everything killed! Still, you know how my warriors are. They thought that they'd bring the best ones back for a sacrifice."

The prophet Samuel just shook his head and said,

"Everything would have been fine if you'd only done what you were told. Instead, you've made God mad, and at this point He wishes that He'd made someone else the King of Israel. Anyone would have been better than you."

Samuel then hacked the King of the Amalekites to pieces himself, and walked away from Saul, never to speak to him again. The prophet Samuel eventually died, and was lamented by all the Israelites.

Saul continued on as king, although God stopped talking to him. Instead, God started grooming a young man named David to take over the job. On a side note, David married Saul's daughter, but not until he fulfilled a task that was assigned to him – bringing King Saul the foreskin of the penis of two hundred men… but that's a different story for another time.

Later on, when the Israelites were attacked by the Philistines, Saul was concerned because he wasn't getting any instructions from God. He decided that if he could only talk to his old friend, the prophet Samuel, he could find out what to do. Of course, the big problem there was that Samuel was dead.

Years before, Saul had driven anyone claiming to have supernatural talents from the land, but he found himself in dire need of someone who could help him talk to Samuel. He sent his servants out to find someone with a "familiar spirit" – who could talk to the dead, in other words – and they came back with word about a woman who lived in the City of Endor that had such powers. Saul disguised himself, put on some ordinary clothes, and went with the two servants to see the woman one evening. He asks her to summon the spirit of a particular person that he is going to name.

Since she didn't know him, she assumed that he was trying to entrap her. She replied, "Hey, you know that King Saul tossed out all the mediums. Are you trying to get me in trouble or something?"

Saul swears to her in God's name that she won't get any in kind of trouble, so she finally agrees to do as he asks. When she requests the name of the deceased to call forward, Saul had one request: "Bring up Samuel."

The woman performed her conjuring, and suddenly Samuel was standing before her. She then realized what was going on, and basically said, "Wait a minute – you're King Saul. Why are you trying to trick me?" Probably a sincere question, since Saul had previously put everyone to death that dealt in the supernatural.

Saul tried to comfort her, saying, "Don't be afraid; just tell me what you saw."

"I saw gods coming up out of the earth," she said. "It looks like an old man wearing a cloak."

Since Saul assumed this to be Samuel, even though he couldn't see him, he bowed down on the ground.

Samuel then addressed Saul. "Why the heck are you disturbing me, and bringing me back here like this?"

"It's because I'm a little worried. The Philistines are attacking, and since God isn't communicating with me anymore, I thought that I'd call you to find out what to do about the upcoming battle."

Samuel must have been a little put out with him. "Don't look for any help from me – you're the one that disobeyed God's orders about the Amalekites. Now he's cut you off, and he's getting David ready to take over your kingdom. And by the way, your army is going to be defeated in battle tomorrow and by the end of the day you and your sons are going to be here with me... you will die."

The prophet disappeared, and Saul collapsed on the ground after he heard the news.

Sure enough, Saul's army was defeated the next day and his sons were killed. Instead of allowing himself to be taken prisoner, he asked his armor-bearer to kill him, but the man refused. Saul then committed suicide by falling on his sword, and the bodies of he and his sons were displayed on the city of Beth-shan's outer wall... and thus ends the saga of Saul.

The incident with the "Witch of Endor," although she's actually more of a medium, has caused a bit of a problem for people through the years. Many say that because ghosts do not – and cannot – exist, the specter must therefore be a demon sent to fool Saul. They point to semantics such as the fact that the medium said she saw, "gods coming up out of the earth," and not down from heaven – of course, "heaven" isn't up in the sky any more than hell is under the ground.

The major issue is that the Bible actually states that the spirit is Samuel in verse 15. Not a demon masquerading as Samuel, not a trick being played by the medium, but Samuel himself. Some try to say that it is only Saul's perception that it is Samuel, but that's simply not what the Bible says – it is, in fact, Samuel. End of discussion.

The other interesting thing is that the spirit tells Saul about the outcome of the battle, even predicting the death of him and his sons... which of course, came true. If it was a demon, then that demon had the gift of prophesy. Since Samuel was a prophet, however, foreseeing the outcome of the battle would not be an issue if God revealed it to him.

Perhaps the biggest problem comes from considering what the purpose of the story would be if the spirit was a demon. If that were the case, the demon: chastised Saul for disobeying God; told Saul that God was raising up a new king, David; and correctly predicted that Saul would not only lose the upcoming battle, but that he and his sons would be killed. The ghost seems to be a herald of God, not a dark force with a demonic agenda. Still, there are those who insist that is the case, for the simple reason that they don't believe that ghosts exist.

Witch of Endor by Nikolai Ge, 1857

According to this passage, 1 Samuel 15:1-3, not only do ghosts exist, but they can communicate with the living, they have knowledge of events in our world, and it is possible for them to be summoned.

Just as an aside, a very interesting thing about this passage of scripture is finally learning where the mother on the television show *Bewitched* got her name... "Endora," taken from the name of the City of Endor, where the witch lived!

Night of the Living Dead, Sans Zombies

There is only one movie that has given me recurring nightmares: George Romero's wonderful horror classic *Night of the Living Dead.* Wow, did that one affect me, and on several different levels. Many a night I've woken up screaming, turning on the lights and jumping out of bed to escape the zombies in my dreams that were stumbling toward me to feast on my innards.

You probably remember the premise to the story – a comet passed too close to the Earth, and mysterious radiation from it brings the dead back to life. They claw their way out of the graves, stumbling mindlessly along in search of one thing... living human flesh! (cue the spooky music here)

Now, you may be wondering why it is that I'm invoking one of Hollywood's horror classics in this book, and it's only because I wanted to mention another aspect of people coming back to Earth in the pages of the Bible – not as ghosts, but as humans.

The most interesting account of this to me is in Matthew 27, verses 51-53:

⁵¹And, behold, the veil of the temple was rent in twain from the top to the bottom; and the earth did quake, and the rocks rent;

⁵²And the graves were opened; and many bodies of the saints which slept arose,

⁵³And came out of the graves after his resurrection, and went into the holy city, and appeared unto many.

Plaque with the saints rising from the dead, Limoges artwork, c. 1250

If you do research on these verses, you'll find them to be a firestorm of controversy. Scholars from different denominations of Christianity can't agree on what really happened, although it is clearly stated: Jesus died, the temple curtain split in half, there was an earthquake that tore boulders apart, and the graves opened up. Many – but not all – of the bodies in the graves arose from the dead, and three days later, emerged after Christ's resurrection. From there, the now-living, previously-dead people went into the city where a lot of folks saw them. Unlike the aforementioned horror movie, however, there is no evidence that they fed on the flesh of humans. Sorry... just thought that I'd throw that one in.

There were previous occurrences of reanimation of the deceased before this, however. I Kings 17:17-24 tells the story of the widow at Zarephath – the prophet Elijah was staying at the house of a widow who had a son. Although she had little food, Elijah had worked a miracle so that they would have plenty to eat during the time that he was there. At one point, the son became ill, and the mother was understandably distraught. Elijah took the body upstairs, laid it out, and then stretched himself over the body three times. He called out, "O Lord my God, I pray thee, let this child's soul come into him again." God heard the prayer, the son was brought back from the dead, and the mom was happy again.

Jesus himself brought another widow's son back to life, as told in Luke 7:11-15. He arrived in the village of Nain in time to see a funeral procession for the only son of a widowed woman. Feeling sorry for her, Jesus looked in the coffin and said, "Young man, I say unto thee, Arise!" The kid sits up and immediately starts talking, and although at most funerals this would totally freak out the congregation, in this case it was instantly recognized as a miracle.

The Apostle Paul even gets in on the bringing-back-the-dead action in Acts 20:9-10. He's preaching in a room of the upper floor of a building in the city of Troas, and as he goes on and on, the sermon stretches all the way to midnight. A man named Eutychus who was sitting on a windowsill began to fall asleep as the time passed, and when he finally dozed off, he tumbled out and fell three stories to his death. Everyone ran downstairs, but Paul laid down on top of the young man and then embraced him. He stood up and told the crowd, "Hey, don't worry... he is alive!" They all went back upstairs, grabbed a quick bite to eat, and then Paul continued preaching until daybreak.

Of course, the story that everyone learned in Sunday School was about a fellow named Lazarus. Jesus was a friend to a family in the city of Bethany – two sisters, Mary and Martha, and their brother Lazarus. When the brother fell ill, the sisters went to find Jesus and told them how worried they were about their brother. The Lord told them not to worry, but hung out where he was a couple of days before going to check on Lazarus. By the time he got there, the guy had died, and had been in the grave four days. As Jesus approached, Martha ran out to meet him and said, "If you had been here, my brother wouldn't have died. Even though he did, though, I know that God's going to give you whatever you ask." Well, to make a long story short, they take Jesus to the grave and he asked that the stone covering it be rolled away. The sisters protest, saying that since he's been dead for four days, the body's going to stink something fierce. They do what Jesus asks, though, and he yells, "Lazarus, come out!" Sure enough, here the fellow comes, still wrapped in the burial shroud – he was brought back to life.

All of the incidents that I just mentioned were with individual dead guys, resurrected by other individuals: Elijah, Paul, and of course, Christ Himself. Only at the crucifixion was there a spontaneous, multiple resurrection. Matthew doesn't tell us what happened to those people that came back from the dead, or why they didn't leave their graves until after Jesus' own resurrection. He just said that it happened.

The reason that I wanted to mention the mass event as well as the individual ones is that the Bible makes it clear that there is a way for the spirit to pass from the next world back into this one, and at least in these cases, back into the body that it once inhabited. If this resurrection can occur, than how much more possible would it be for a spirit to simply come back for a visit?

Jesus Describes Ghosts

I think that the definitive word on the subject of ghosts for me would be the words of Jesus Christ. In my theology, He is the risen Son of the living God, and He provides the path to salvation from an eternal damnation… so one has to wonder what someone so important has to say about ghosts.

If such spirits were evil, He would certainly espouse terrible things about them. After all, the Lord wasn't bashful when it came to such things. Take, for example, Matthew 21, when Jesus went to the temple and found that dealers were exchanging the standard Greek and Roman coin for Jewish and Tyrian, which were the only coinage that could be used in the temple ceremonies. The dealers were also selling doves and other sacrificial animals, and making quite a profit.

What did Christ do? Well, He basically got mad, as we see in Matthew 21:12-14…

[12]And Jesus went into the temple of God, and cast out all them that sold and bought in the temple, and overthrew the tables of the moneychangers, and the seats of them that sold doves,

91

¹³*And said unto them, It is written, My house shall be called the house of prayer; but ye have made it a den of thieves.*

¹⁴*And the blind and the lame came to him in the temple; and he healed them.*

This account is in all four gospels, and I encourage you to read it in each. As you'll see in other accounts, he actually made a whip out of some cords, and physically beat the moneychangers out of the temple. This is someone who doesn't mess around – he says what he thinks, and he always sticks to his guns regarding what is right, and what is wrong.

After his death, however, Luke 24:36-43 gives the following account of Jesus' appearance to his disciples. They had been to the empty tomb, and were standing in the village of Emmaus discussing the situation when suddenly the Lord was standing there with them:

³⁶*And as they thus spake, Jesus himself stood in the midst of them, and saith unto them, Peace be unto you.*

³⁷*But they were terrified and affrighted, and supposed that they had seen a spirit.*

³⁸*And he said unto them, Why are ye troubled? and why do thoughts arise in your hearts?*

³⁹*Behold my hands and my feet, that it is I myself: handle me, and see; for a spirit hath not flesh and bones, as ye see me have.*

⁴⁰*And when he had thus spoken, he shewed them his hands and his feet.*

⁴¹*And while they yet believed not for joy, and wondered, he said unto them, Have ye here any meat?*

^{42}And they gave him a piece of a broiled fish, and of an honeycomb.

^{43}And he took it, and did eat before them.

This is very much like the time that Jesus was walking on the water and the disciples thought he was a ghost. In this case, though, they had seen him brutally executed on the cross and his body placed in a mountainside tomb sealed with a heavy rock. There was just no question – Jesus was dead.

Yet here they were standing around talking, and up walks Jesus with a greeting of their day: "Peace be unto you." If this took place in our world today, he might step into their group and say, "What up?" just like I'd do when approaching a circle of my friends.

The disciples weren't just startled, the scripture says that they were "terrified and affrighted, and supposed that they had seen a spirit."

If their reaction had been blasphemous to Jesus, I don't think that he would have had a problem with calling them out on it – remember the verses about the temple moneychangers in the verses that I quoted a bit ago? Instead, he didn't seem to find this offensive at all. Instead, he gently corrected them by explaining that it really was him, and then showing them the crucifixion marks on his hands and his feet.

He then does something even more interesting... he goes on to explain the attributes of a ghost. He says, "A spirit doesn't have any flesh and bones, but you see that I do." He then asked for something to eat – another thing that a ghost wouldn't be able to do.

This passage is most powerful because it tells of the

resurrection of Jesus, but in a secondary way I find it to be interesting because the Lord himself not only acknowledges that spirits exist, but goes on to actually describe them to the disciples… and to us!

To be honest, I can't think of a better resource for such information than Christ when He was here on Earth.

Jesus Appears to His Disciples by Alexandre Bida, c. 1873

Section 6: Other Paranormal Topics in the Bible

"Paranormal" is defined as outside of the normal, or beyond the scope of present-day, scientific understanding or proof. Prior to the Wright brothers, we would have classified flight by man in that category.

Along with having all the information about ghosts that we looked at in the previous chapter, the Bible also touches on some topics that might just surprise you.

I wanted to mention just a few of them here because the Bible gets such a terrible rap – it's often viewed as a judgmental hammer that people use against each other, when in reality it is an incredible and interesting resource.

Don't get me wrong – these things are very controversial in the world of religion. Some people spend time arguing about them, while others deal with by them by simply ignoring the fact that they exist. Either case makes them all the more intriguing, though. If you take the time to delve into its mysteries, you just might find that the Bible is something that is quite fascinating…

Astral Projection

You may remember from the previous discussion about "giving up the ghost" that when a person dies, their spirit leaves the body and continues on in another form of existence with those who have passed before him. Recall that Genesis 49:33 says:

> [33]*And when Jacob had made an end of commanding his sons, he gathered up his feet into the bed, and yielded up the ghost, and was gathered unto his people.*

There are, however, reports of people whose spirit is able to leave the body, travel about (sometimes great distances), and then return back to the body. In our world this is commonly known as Astral Projection, Out of Body Experiences, Soul Travel, or Spirit Walking – pick the name that you like best, but we'll stick to the first one just for the purposes of this discussion.

As it turns out, this isn't an uncommon experience. British psychologist Susan Blackmore did a survey of a population in England and found that a full twelve percent of those in the study had experienced Astral Projection. Her findings were published in the *Skeptical Enquirer* magazine, but were not surprising. Other studies report from eight percent to fifty percent, depending on the particular focus group.

This concept also appears in the Bible, which contains instances where the living travel through Astral Projection, or as the Scriptures say, "in spirit." In most cases a guide takes the traveler to distant lands or even realms beyond Earth, and shows them things that are unknown to them.

96

Consider, for example, the Apostle Paul's words in 2 Corinthians, Chapter 12...

¹It is not expedient for me doubtless to glory. I will come to visions and revelations of the Lord.
²I knew a man in Christ above fourteen years ago, (whether in the body, I cannot tell; or whether out of the body, I cannot tell: God knoweth;) such an one caught up to the third heaven.
³And I knew such a man, (whether in the body, or out of the body, I cannot tell: God knoweth;)
⁴How that he was caught up into paradise, and heard unspeakable words, which it is not lawful for a man to utter.
⁵Of such an one will I glory: yet of myself I will not glory, but in mine infirmities.

Most folks believe that Paul was relating his own experience, referring to himself as "a man in Christ." What he is basically saying is that fourteen years ago he was taken up to heaven to look around. The interesting thing is that he says, "But don't ask me whether my body was there, or it was just my spirit. I really don't know, but God does." This fact is so important that he mentions it twice, before saying that he was in paradise and heard things so amazing that they couldn't be described – not that he would be allowed to do so even if he could.

Although some try to write this off as a dream, Paul believes that either 1) he was physically there with his body, or 2) just his spirit was taken there. A dream isn't one of the options that he considers.

Paul had quite a few experiences with Astral

Projection, as it turns out. Not only with his own spirit going places, but with the spirit of someone that was alive and living in Macedonia coming to talk to him. The story is told in Acts 16:

⁹And a vision appeared to Paul in the night; There stood a man of Macedonia, and prayed him, saying, Come over into Macedonia, and help us.
¹⁰And after he had seen the vision, immediately we endeavoured to go into Macedonia, assuredly gathering that the Lord had called us for to preach the gospel unto them.

In this case, Paul was shown a vision of a man from Macedonia, who pleaded for help. The Bible doesn't say that it was a man that looked like he might have come from Macedonia, or a man who told Paul that he was from Macedonia... no, it is clear that before Paul stood, "a man of Macedonia." Although some might argue that Paul had merely had a dream where a message was revealed to him, that's not what the Bible says – and the description of the event certainly fits the case where the Macedonian man was Astral Projecting.

Paul isn't the only one to do a bit of Astral Projecting, however. Let's look to the Prophet Ezekiel and an encounter he had that is told in Ezekiel 8:

¹And it came to pass in the sixth year, in the sixth month, in the fifth day of the month, as I sat in mine house, and the elders of Judah sat before me, that the hand of the Lord GOD fell there upon me.

²Then I beheld, and lo a likeness as the appearance of fire: from the appearance of his loins even downward, fire; and from his loins even upward, as the appearance of brightness, as the colour of amber.

³And he put forth the form of an hand, and took me by a lock of mine head; and the spirit lifted me up between the earth and the heaven, and brought me in the visions of God to Jerusalem, to the door of the inner gate that looketh toward the north; where was the seat of the image of jealousy, which provoketh to jealousy.

⁴And, behold, the glory of the God of Israel was there, according to the vision that I saw in the plain.

At the first of this chapter, Ezekiel is sitting in his house, and the Elders of Judah were sitting there waiting to hear what he had to say. A heavenly being – the form of Christ, some say – appears before him as a figure of fire. The Lord touches a lock of his hair, and Ezekiel is led to Jerusalem, to the north gate of the temple, where he is shown many things. After quite a long tour of different places and people, the prophet is returned as explained in Ezekiel 11:

²⁴Afterwards the Spirit of God carried me back again to Babylon, to the Jews in exile there. And so ended the vision of my visit to Jerusalem.

²⁵And I told the exiles everything the Lord had shown me.

To the Elders sitting there in his home, it may have appeared that Ezekiel had entered some kind of trance, or was in deep meditation, because only his spirit was taken on the long journey, and then returned to the body, in what can only be described as an Out of Body Experience, or Astral Projection.

In the Book of Revelation, John is taken on an incredible voyage through Heaven, and shown many prophetic things. Many call this a dream, but here is what the Book of Revelation, Chapter 1 actually says:

⁹I John, who also am your brother, and companion in tribulation, and in the kingdom and patience of Jesus Christ, was in the isle that is called Patmos, for the word of God, and for the testimony of Jesus Christ.

¹⁰I was in the Spirit on the Lord's day, and heard behind me a great voice, as of a trumpet,

¹¹Saying, I am Alpha and Omega, the first and the last: and, What thou seest, write in a book, and send it unto the seven churches which are in Asia; unto Ephesus, and unto Smyrna, and unto Pergamos, and unto Thyatira, and unto Sardis, and unto Philadelphia, and unto Laodicea.

¹²And I turned to see the voice that spake with me. And being turned, I saw seven golden candlesticks;

¹³And in the midst of the seven candlesticks one like unto the Son of man, clothed with a garment down to the foot, and girt about the paps with a golden girdle.

¹⁴His head and his hairs were white like wool, as white as snow; and his eyes were as a flame of fire;

¹⁵And his feet like unto fine brass, as if they burned in a furnace; and his voice as the sound of many waters.

Notice that in Verse 10, John says "I was in the Spirit…" That's the first of four times in the Book of

Revelation that he uses that terminology. The second is in Revelation 4:2:

And immediately I was in the spirit: and, behold, a throne was set in heaven, and one sat on the throne.

Here John is shown the glorious throne-room of God. The phrase is used a third time in Revelation 17:3, which says,

So he carried me away in the Spirit into the wilderness. And I saw a woman sitting on a scarlet beast which was full of names of blasphemy, having seven heads and ten horns.

In this passage John is being shown Babylon. The final occurrence is in Revelation 21:10 –

And he carried me away in the Spirit to a great and high mountain, and showed me the great city, the holy Jerusalem, descending out of heaven from God.

John's spirit is taken to many places and shown beautiful – and chilling – things. In Revelation 22:8, he concludes by saying:

And I John saw these things, and heard them.

John didn't dream them; he actually witnessed them, while being escorted about in spirit form… and that's the very definition of Astral Projection.

Giants and the Sons of God

I think one of the most baffling passages in the entire Bible comes from Genesis 6. It takes place after the creation, but before the Great Flood. Before going any further, take a look at versus 1-4:

¹And it came to pass, when men began to multiply on the face of the earth, and daughters were born unto them,
²That the sons of God saw the daughters of men that they were fair; and they took them wives of all which they chose.
³And the Lord said, My spirit shall not always strive with man, for that he also is flesh: yet his days shall be an hundred and twenty years.
⁴There were giants in the earth in those days; and also after that, when the sons of God came in unto the daughters of men, and they bore children to them, the same became mighty men which were of old, men of renown.

There are two interesting things in those four verses. The first is the term "sons of God." Clearly, whatever beings being referred to are different from man. Look at verse 1, which says "men began to multiply" and "daughters were born unto them." The very next verse says that the "sons of God" saw the "daughters of men" and thought that they were beautiful, and picked out the ones that they wanted for wives.

This is a very interesting topic to research online – just do a web search for "sons of God" and Genesis. There are many, many theories from the sons of God simply being men of one tribe or another, to them being angels, or even aliens. There's a lot of scrambling to try to explain these puzzling few verses, and most of the information is confusing and contradictory between the scholars.

I just know that to me, there are beings called "sons of God" that were mating with human females, and the scripture certainly doesn't sound like the sons were ordinary men. Fascinating.

The other thing about this passage is the mention of giants. Verse four begins with, "There were giants in the earth in those days..." Contrast that to the first verse, which says, "...men began to multiply on the face of the earth..." There is one difference that intrigues me:

*"men **on** the earth" vs. "giants **in** the earth"*

I have to wonder about "on versus "in." Why wouldn't the writer of Genesis Chapter 6 (whoever that might be, which is another topic by itself) use the same terminology within the scope of four small verses?

To me, it clearly states that there were men living *on* the face – or surface – of the earth, and there were giants living *in* the earth. Think about that one for a moment.

There are other descriptions of giants in the Bible, though. I'm going to list several of the verses, and I encourage you to open your Bible and read them in context. You'll find the idea of races of giants in Old Testament times isn't that radical of an idea.

The Book of Amos, Chapter 2, talks about huge beings:

[9]Yet destroyed I the Amorite before them, whose height was like the height of the cedars, and he was strong

as the oaks; yet I destroyed his fruit from above, and his roots from beneath.

[10]Also I brought you up from the land of Egypt, and led you forty years through the wilderness, to possess the land of the Amorite.

The second chapter of the book of Deuteronomy talks about giants as well:

[10]The Emims dwelt therein in times past, a people great, and many, and tall, as the Anakims;
[11]Which also were accounted giants, as the Anakims; but the Moabites called them Emims.

Later in Deuteronomy 2, verses 19 through 21 say:

¹⁹And when thou comest nigh over against the children of Ammon, distress them not, nor meddle with them: for I will not give thee of the land of the children of Ammon any possession; because I have given it unto the children of Lot for a possession.

²⁰(That also was accounted a land of giants: giants dwelt therein in old time; and the Ammonites call them Zamzummims;

²¹A people great, and many, and tall, as the Anakims; but the Lord destroyed them before them; and they succeeded them, and dwelt in their stead.

Deuteronomy 3 actually gives the size of a giant's bed (specifically Og, the King of Bashan, the last of the giants). His bed was 9 cubits long, but four cubits wide. That translates to 13.5 feet long by 6 feet wide – that's much larger than a standard king-size bed, which is about 6.5 feet long by 6 feet wide (I measured the one that my wife and I sleep in). The difference is that two people sleep in my bed, but only Og slept in his, which was 7 feet longer than mine. Now *that's* a giant; but here's the verse:

¹¹For only Og king of Bashan remained of the remnant of giants; behold his bedstead was a bedstead of iron; is it not in Rabbath of the children of Ammon? nine cubits was the length thereof, and four cubits the breadth of it, after the cubit of a man.

Of course, there is also the giant named Goliath that David killed with a rock and a slingshot, which is described in 1 Samuel 17. The point is, though, that the Bible seems to clearly talk about races of giants that are much larger than normal man.

And I still can't forget about Genesis 6 that we looked at earlier, which says: *There were giants in the earth in those days...*

Unicorns in the Bible

I have friends who are cryptozoologists; that is to say, they study animals whose existence has not been scientifically proven. This field of study includes creatures like sasquatch (a.k.a. bigfoot, yeti, or any of its other monikers), sea creatures like the Loch Ness Monster, the ferocious little chupacabra, and other strange beings of lore such as the MothMan.

I've never heard of these friends of mine looking for a unicorn, however, yet there is documentation in the Bible indicating that it was not a mythical creature, but instead a living, breathing animal.

The unicorns of the Bible don't fly or even have wings. They don't work magic and their blood doesn't perpetuate youth or heal the sick; they are simply described as being just another animal.

Like any other fringe topic in the Bible, the idea of unicorns has been greatly debated. Some feel that the mention of such creatures discredits the Bible and makes it laughable, and they therefore go to great lengths to explain the animal as one common to our world.

For me, the Bible says "unicorn," and so I have to believe that at least at one time, such a creature existed. There are a number of verses in the Bible that talk about them.

The Hunt of the Unicorn, circa 1495

First let's consider Job 39, where God is humbling Job by talking to him about various animals:

¹Knowest thou the time when the wild goats of the rock bring forth? or canst thou mark when the hinds do calve?

²Canst thou number the months that they fulfil? or knowest thou the time when they bring forth?

³They bow themselves, they bring forth their young ones, they cast out their sorrows.

⁴Their young ones are in good liking, they grow up with corn; they go forth, and return not unto them.

⁵Who hath sent out the wild ass free? or who hath loosed the bands of the wild ass?

107

⁶Whose house I have made the wilderness, and the barren land his dwellings.

⁷He scorneth the multitude of the city, neither regardeth he the crying of the driver.

⁸The range of the mountains is his pasture, and he searcheth after every green thing.

⁹Will the unicorn be willing to serve thee, or abide by thy crib?

¹⁰Canst thou bind the unicorn with his band in the furrow? or will he harrow the valleys after thee?

¹¹Wilt thou trust him, because his strength is great? or wilt thou leave thy labour to him?

¹²Wilt thou believe him, that he will bring home thy seed, and gather it into thy barn?

¹³Gavest thou the goodly wings unto the peacocks? or wings and feathers unto the ostrich?

¹⁴Which leaveth her eggs in the earth, and warmeth them in dust,

¹⁵And forgetteth that the foot may crush them, or that the wild beast may break them.

The most interesting thing about this passage to me is that the unicorns are being mentioned in simple context with several other everyday animals: goats, donkeys, peacocks, etc. People don't doubt any of those creatures, because you can seem them in any zoo. The unicorn has been brought into the fantasy literature genre, however, so its mention is often discredited so that the Bible won't seem, well, silly.

There is more scripture to look at, however. Look at the Book of Numbers, Chapter 23, Verse 22:

²²God brought them out of Egypt; he hath as it were the strength of a unicorn.

If you were to delete "unicorn" and substitute the word "Clydesdale," people would have no trouble at all reading the verse – after all, a Clydesdale is an extremely powerful animal.

Psalms 22 also mentions the beast:

²⁰Deliver my soul from the sword; my darling from the power of the dog.
²¹Save me from the lion's mouth: for thou hast heard me from the horns of the unicorns.

There it talks about other animals in conjunction with the unicorn; specifically, dogs and lions. There are other mentions of the unicorn in the Bible, but they all mention it in a very casual sense – just as if we would talk about a horse today.

Personally I don't have a problem with unicorns. Various species of animals disappear every year; just try to find a Dodo Bird today, for example. The human race isn't known for making Earth conducive to animal life.

Just the opposite, in fact.

The other argument against unicorns is that a full skeleton has never been discovered – yet every year a new kind of dinosaur is unearthed that has never been seen before. Who knows, perhaps a perfectly preserved unicorn skeleton will be next.

In a strange twist, in 2012 the North Korean Central News Agency (KCNA) reported that a unicorn's lair had been discovered from ancient times.

Lair of King Tongmyong's Unicorn Reconfirmed in DPRK

Pyongyang, November 29 (KCNA) -- Archaeologists of the History Institute of the DPRK Academy of Social Sciences have recently reconfirmed a lair of the unicorn rode by King Tongmyong, founder of the Koguryo Kingdom (B.C. 277-A.D. 668).

The lair is located 200 meters from the Yongmyong Temple in Moran Hill in Pyongyang City. A rectangular rock carved with words "Unicorn Lair" stands in front of the lair. The carved words are believed to date back to the period of Koryo Kingdom (918-1392).

Jo Hui Sung, director of the Institute, told KCNA:

"Korea's history books deal with the unicorn, considered to be ridden by King Tongmyong, and its lair.

The Sogyong (Pyongyang) chapter of the old book 'Koryo History' (geographical book), said: Ulmil Pavilion is on the top of Mt. Kumsu, with Yongmyong Temple, one of Pyongyang's eight scenic spots, beneath it. The temple served as a relief palace for King Tongmyong, in which there is the

---

Beginning Text of the KCNA News Release

Most reporters had a great time poking fun at the news release, but who knows – if unicorns existed in Biblical times, perhaps there was merit to their discovery.

In the mean time, I simply like to sing the lyrics of that old song by the Irish Rovers, *The Unicorn*:

A long time ago, when the Earth was green,
There was more kinds of animals than you've ever seen.
And they'd run around free when the Earth was born,
And the loveliest of 'em all was the unicorn...

Monsters in the Bible

With all the talk about unicorns in the Bible, it might not surprise you to learn that there is talk of monsters as well. Take, for instance, this passage from Revelation 12 talking about a dragon:

110

³And there appeared another wonder in heaven; and behold a great red dragon, having seven heads and ten horns, and seven crowns upon his heads.

The book of Revelation is accepted to be the vision that was given to a man named John (although *which* John is a subject of debate). It's full of monstrous creatures including a leviathan, a behemoth, and a few dragons.

In many passages it is clear that in the vision the dragon is a symbol for Satan. But why use a comparison with no factual basis? As creationist author and filmmaker Darek Isaacs observed, "If dragons in fact were entirely mythological, if they were a figment of the imagination, and if they never ever did exist, then God just compared our adversary to a make-believe creature that never existed."

Dragons also appear in the book of Psalms, as they do in Chapter 91:

¹³Thou shalt tread upon the lion and adder: the young lion and the dragon shalt thou trample under feet.

...and then again in chapter 74:

¹³Thou didst divide the sea by thy strength: thou brakest the heads of the dragons in the waters.

When Deuteronomy 32 is talking about people who have turned away from God, it says:

³³Their wine is the poison of dragons, and the cruel venom of asps.

111

Nehemiah 2 gives a reference to a well named after dragons:

[13] And I went out by night by the gate of the valley, even before the dragon well, and to the dung port, and viewed the walls of Jerusalem, which were broken down, and the gates thereof were consumed with fire.

And dragons even show up in the Book of Job, chapter 30:

[29] I am a brother to dragons, and a companion to owls.

There are more references to dragons, and as a mythical beast involved in fantasy literature, it is a problem for many believers. Some say that they were inspired by great serpents such as Kimono Dragons, others contend that they were just fanciful references. Whatever the case, the Bible has many more than are listed here – which makes me wonder just how mythical this creature really is.

Another with almost as much press-time in the Scriptures is the Leviathan, a fierce sea monster.

The Book of Job, Chapter 41 completely describes the fire-breathing Leviathan. Here's just a portion of it:

[14] Who can open the doors of his face? his teeth are terrible round about.

[15] His scales are his pride, shut up together as with a close seal.

[16] One is so near to another, that no air can come between them.

[17]They are joined one to another, they stick together, that they cannot be sundered.

[18]By his neesings a light doth shine, and his eyes are like the eyelids of the morning.

[19]Out of his mouth go burning lamps, and sparks of fire leap out.

[20]Out of his nostrils goeth smoke, as out of a seething pot or caldron.

[21]His breath kindleth coals, and a flame goeth out of his mouth.

[22]In his neck remaineth strength, and sorrow is turned into joy before him.

[23]The flakes of his flesh are joined together: they are firm in themselves; they cannot be moved.

[24]His heart is as firm as a stone; yea, as hard as a piece of the nether millstone.

The Book of Isaiah, Chapter 27 says this:

[1]In that day the LORD with his sore and great and strong sword shall punish leviathan the piercing serpent, even leviathan that crooked serpent; and he shall slay the dragon that [is] in the sea.

Psalms even talks about a Leviathan, and "dragons in the waters," in Chapter 74:

[12]For God is my King of old, working salvation in the midst of the earth.

[13]Thou didst divide the sea by thy strength: thou brakest the heads of the dragons in the waters.

14Thou brakest the heads of leviathan in pieces, and gavest him to be meat to the people inhabiting the wilderness.

Destruction of Leviathan, 1865 engraving by Gustave Doré

While we could go on about the Leviathan, before leaving the monsters of the Bible it's worth mentioning the Behemoth. Job 40 describes this beast, and the problem in explaining this monster away is that in this passage of Scripture, it is actually God talking to Job. He starts out by basically saying, "Hey, check out the behemoth, which I created when I created man…"

¹⁵ Behold now behemoth, which I made with thee; he eateth grass as an ox.

¹⁶ Lo now, his strength is in his loins, and his force is in the navel of his belly.

¹⁷ He moveth his tail like a cedar: the sinews of his stones are wrapped together.

¹⁸ His bones are as strong pieces of brass; his bones are like bars of iron.

¹⁹ He is the chief of the ways of God: he that made him can make his sword to approach unto him.

²⁰ Surely the mountains bring him forth food, where all the beasts of the field play.

²¹ He lieth under the shady trees, in the covert of the reed, and fens.

²² The shady trees cover him with their shadow; the willows of the brook compass him about.

²³ Behold, he drinketh up a river, and hasteth not: he trusteth that he can draw up Jordan into his mouth.

²⁴ He taketh it with his eyes: his nose pierceth through snares.

Some have hypothesized that the Behemoth might actually be a dinosaur, but ignoring the carbon dating of dino-bones and ancient-man bones, the scripture says in verse 16 that he has a bellybutton – that would mean that he was not hatched from an egg like dinosaurs were, but instead was live-born.

There are many creatures that modern-day man has never, and will never, see for himself. According to the Bible, dragons, leviathans and behemoths are just a few. Personally, I find that to be very, very interesting.

Reincarnation in the Bible

Reincarnation seems like such a foreign topic when you're mentioning the Bible. Some people, however, believe that the Holy Scripture actually proves that reincarnation exists. You may remember the story of the Transfiguration that we looked at earlier, where three of the disciples saw Jesus talking to Moses and Elijah on the top of a mountain.

Let's pick up that story as Christ and the disciples were walking down the mountain:

[9]*And as they came down from the mountain, Jesus charged them, saying, Tell the vision to no man, until the Son of man be risen again from the dead.*

[10]*And his disciples asked him, saying, Why then say the scribes that Elias must first come?*

[11]*And Jesus answered and said unto them, Elias truly shall first come, and restore all things.*

[12]*But I say unto you, That Elias is come already, and they knew him not, but have done unto him whatsoever they listed. Likewise shall also the Son of man suffer of them.*

[13]*Then the disciples understood that he spoke to them of John the Baptist.*

Things at that point had become even more interesting. As they're heading back down the mountain, Jesus warned them not to tell anyone until after he has arisen from the dead. The disciples point out that the scribes have always said that the prophet Elijah had to come before that happened.

Jesus agrees that Elijah had to come first, but added

that in fact, the prophet had already come – it's just that no one recognized him, although they killed him. Jesus then informed them that the same thing was going to happen to him.

The Bible clearly states that at that point, as they continued on, the disciples realized that Jesus was saying that John the Baptist had been Elijah.

This Elijah/John the Baptist connection is often quoted to support the idea of reincarnation.

I've read dozens of interpretations of this passage, and they all pretty much come down to people bending it to support their individual beliefs. Those who believe in reincarnation point out that Jesus does say that Elijah has come back to Earth, but the people didn't recognize him as such – because he came back in the form of John the Baptist. Others refute this, dismissing it with flawed logic such as, "since reincarnation isn't true, John the Baptist couldn't have been Elijah."

John the Baptist himself dismissed the idea that he was Elijah in John 1:21:

21And they asked him, What then? Art thou Elias? And he saith, I am not. Art thou that prophet? And he answered, No.

Jesus seems to give another idea about it, though, in Matthew 11, where he is talking about John and says,

13For all the prophets and the law prophesied until John.
14And if ye will receive it, this is Elias, which was for to come.

117

[15]*He that hath ears to hear, let him hear.*

Both opponents and proponents of reincarnation take both of those two statements, John the Baptist's and Jesus' respectively, to support their individual ideas – one way or the other.

People who believe in reincarnation typically find that John the Baptist's statement is rational, because within their belief system, you usually have no clue who you were in a previous life. John the Baptist would therefore perceive himself only as John the Baptist, and his proclamation as such would make perfect sense. Jesus, on the other hand, would have divine knowledge as the Son of God and could therefore definitively state that John the Baptist had actually been Elijah returned.

But it is also important, however, to note that the transfiguration passage doesn't say that Jesus directly admitted that John the Baptist was Elijah; it only states that the disciples had the understanding (for right or wrong, possibly) that he had been speaking of John the Baptist.

Still others have an even more interesting interpretation of the John/Elijah relationship, using the fact that Elijah never actually died – he was borne up to heaven by a whirlwind, as told in 2 Kings 2:11 – and therefore could still be interpreted as being alive, and simply existing in some other form until reappearing back on Earth as John the Baptist, and then dying as him. Since Luke 1 describes the birth of John the Baptist, though, it isn't as though Elijah could have just beamed back to Earth as a grown man and assumed the persona of John. There would have had to have been a moving of the spirit from Elijah's body which was taken directly to heaven into the little baby that was born to the old man Zechariah and his sterile wife Elizabeth.

There are other mentions of this possible reincarnation in the Bible. In Mark 8. Jesus inquires of his disciples what the people were saying about him, as follows in verses 27-30:

[27] And Jesus went out, and his disciples, into the towns of Caesarea Philippi: and by the way he asked his disciples, saying unto them, Whom do men say that I am?
[28] And they answered, John the Baptist; but some say, Elias; and others, One of the prophets.
[29] And he saith unto them, But whom say ye that I am? And Peter answereth and saith unto him, Thou art the Christ.
[30] And he charged them that they should tell no man of him.

So at least some of the people were saying that Jesus was John the Baptist who had come again, or the prophet Elijah. While He wasn't either one of them, it shows that the notion of reincarnation was something that was regarded as a possibility by people in Biblical times.

In Mark 6, we find that even King Herod seemed to believe in reincarnation. This passage talks about Jesus, from Herod's point of view:

[14] And king Herod heard of him; (for his name was spread abroad:) and he said, That John the Baptist was risen from the dead, and therefore mighty works do shew forth themselves in him.

119

[15]Others said, That it is Elias. And others said, That it is a prophet, or as one of the prophets.

[16]But when Herod heard thereof, he said, It is John, whom I beheaded: he is risen from the dead.

Who knows; an entire book could be written about that one topic alone, and the implications in regard to reincarnation are certainly outside the scope of this one.

Still, it is very interesting to consider.

UFOs in the Bible

I doubt that anyone would argue the existence of UFOs in the Bible – after all, most people have seen a UFO.

What is a UFO? Well, by definition it is simply an Unidentified Flying Object. It doesn't have to be an alien craft. A person might see something moving across the sky out of the corner of their eye, and turn their head to find that it has moved behind a stand of trees. If that person wonders whether it was a bird or an airplane, then the object remains technically unidentified, even though it was almost certainly an everyday object. Still, the observer saw a UFO.

The Bible has things that float, fly and hover in the air that, at least according to their descriptions, are UFOs. Some people believe that they are visions given to those relating the accounts, others believe that they are the manifestations of heavenly beings strange to us on Earth, while still others are convinced that they are an attempt to describe some type of encounters with an alien race.

Personally, I don't have an opinion – but I find the debate to be interesting to consider.

One of the passages quoted most often is Ezekiel's "wheel within a wheel" hovering in the air. It can be found in the first chapter of Ezekiel; here are verses 4-19:

⁴And I looked, and, behold, a whirlwind came out of the north, a great cloud, and a fire infolding itself, and a brightness was about it, and out of the midst thereof as the colour of amber, out of the midst of the fire.

⁵Also out of the midst thereof came the likeness of four living creatures. And this was their appearance; they had the likeness of a man.

⁶And every one had four faces, and every one had four wings.

⁷And their feet were straight feet; and the sole of their feet was like the sole of a calf's foot: and they sparkled like the colour of burnished brass.

⁸And they had the hands of a man under their wings on their four sides; and they four had their faces and their wings.

⁹Their wings were joined one to another; they turned not when they went; they went every one straight forward.

¹⁰As for the likeness of their faces, they four had the face of a man, and the face of a lion, on the right side: and they four had the face of an ox on the left side; they four also had the face of an eagle.

¹¹Thus were their faces: and their wings were stretched upward; two wings of every one were joined one to another, and two covered their bodies.

¹²And they went every one straight forward: whither the spirit was to go, they went; and they turned not when they went.

¹³As for the likeness of the living creatures, their

appearance was like burning coals of fire, and like the appearance of lamps: it went up and down among the living creatures; and the fire was bright, and out of the fire went forth lightning.

[14]And the living creatures ran and returned as the appearance of a flash of lightning.

[15]Now as I beheld the living creatures, behold one wheel upon the earth by the living creatures, with his four faces.

[16]The appearance of the wheels and their work was like unto the colour of a beryl: and they four had one likeness: and their appearance and their work was as it were a wheel in the middle of a wheel.

[17]When they went, they went upon their four sides: and they turned not when they went.

[18]As for their rings, they were so high that they were dreadful; and their rings were full of eyes round about them four.

[19]And when the living creatures went, the wheels went by them: and when the living creatures were lifted up from the earth, the wheels were lifted up.

There's a lot going on not just in that passage, but in the entire first book of Ezekiel.

Verse four says that Ezekiel saw a whirlwind come out of the north with a huge cloud containing a bright light like a fire that was flashing, and out of the light came an amber object. It's not hard to imagine that entire scene looking a lot like the appearance of a spaceship in Spielberg's movie *Close Encounters of the Third Kind*.

The whole affair gets stranger, though. Ezekiel then describes that from the center of the cloud came four strange forms that looked like men, but each had four faces and two pairs of wings. Their legs were described as being similar to those of men, but their feet were cloven like calves' feet, and shone like bright metal. Beneath each of their wings Ezekiel could see something like human hands.

Ezekiel's Chariot Vision, by Matthaeus Merian (1670)

While the human-like legs could be the landing legs of the craft – shining like metal, with shock-absorbing footpads – the rest of the description is quite strange. It goes on to describe faces, wings and other features.

Suddenly, the description takes a very mechanical turn: Ezekiel said that he saw four wheels on the ground beneath them, one wheel belonging to each of the forms, and the wheels seemed to be a shining metal. Not only that, but each wheel was constructed with a second wheel crosswise inside – they could go in any of the four directions without having to turn around. The four wheels had rims and spokes, and the rims were filled with "eyes" around their edges, which some speculate could be portholes or windows.

It is curious that the prophet goes from such an organic description of the object or craft, to a mechanical one with actual wheels.

Ezekiel understood wheels, so they fit easily into his reality. The other components he could have been trying to describe in the only manner that he could – that of beasts, and men.

There are definitely cases where people encountered technology that was so far above their comprehension that they could not begin to grasp it. Take, for example, several South Pacific Island tribes during World War II. The natives reportedly saw airplanes making airdrops of supplies to the troops that had made a temporary base on their island. The military often shared some of the supplies with the islanders, which meant drastic changes to their lifestyle, many of whom had never seen outsiders before. Manufactured clothing, medicine, canned food, tents, weapons and other goods arrived in vast quantities. When the war ended, the military left and the supplies stopped coming.

With their limited understanding of modern technology, the islanders reasoned that the soldiers must be people with a special connection to the gods to get such wonderful supplies. With no concept of air flight, they thought that airplanes must be some conveyance of the gods, so they constructed wood-and-straw airplanes to try to lure back the real ones from the gods. Landing strips and "control towers" were also emulated using local materials.

If one of the natives had sat down to write down a description of airplanes and the air-dropping of supplies, it might have sounded as unbelievable as Ezekiel's depiction of the object that he saw.

There are other passages that people point to as possible evidence of spacecraft in the Bible – the pillar of fire leading the Israelites, the fiery chariot that took Elijah into heaven, and many more.

The real point is that the possibility of flying crafts in the Bible makes it all the more intriguing to explore.

The Supernatural Bible

In this chapter we've gone beyond the idea of ghosts in the Bible, and taken an introductory look at the other supernatural things that it has to offer… but these are just the beginning.

Imagine a man named Jonah who was able to survive for three days after being swallowed by a whale (check out the book of Jonah, chapter 1), or a talking donkey found in Numbers chapter 22, or even a story where Jesus Himself saved a party that had run out of wine in the book of John, chapter 2.

As it turns out, the entire Bible is full of supernatural events, but so are our lives. I love the quote by American clergyman S. Parkes Cadman, "We can see a thousand miracles around us every day. What is more supernatural than an egg yolk turning into a chicken?"

And that's true – the idea of man flying is fairly

recent, in the overall scheme of history. The idea was absurd throughout time until the Wright brothers first flew their airplane at Kitty Hawk, NC on December 17, 1903. Before that time, only witches were credited with the ability to fly, and it was considered to be something so impossible that it was evil. Today, of course, we fly not only in airplanes but in hang gliders, parasails, space shuttles, and any number of other contraptions. We think nothing of it, but there was a time when it was "supernatural."

And what of our universe? Most scientists consider it to be infinite, yet such a concept is not measurable or provable in a laboratory. It's something that most people accept without question, however.

Both birds and butterflies migrate every year without maps or radar, but we have no problem accepting such a thing that is far beyond human ability or understanding.

I was at a party recently, and the subject of domestic animals being able to traverse long distances to find their way home was brought up in conversation. An amazing number of people had stories where a dog or cat had made their way over many miles to find their way to their owners. Personally, I have a friend whose cat was literally kidnapped and taken about fifteen miles away, yet in only a few days' time the cat returned home. That's a factual story, and it has happened so many times to so many people that we don't give it a second thought. But stop and consider it – if that isn't supernatural, then what is?

If our everyday lives are that supernatural, then why shouldn't the Bible be just as interesting? I think that by opening it up and looking inside, you'll find that it is.

126

Section 7: To Sum It All Up…

So, after this examination of what the Bible has to say on the subject of ghosts (and a few other interesting things), exactly what do we know? Well, according to the Scripture, a few things are certain…

1) When we die, our soul (or spirit, or ghost, whatever you would like to call it) leaves our body and joins our loved ones who have gone on before us. (Genesis 25:8)

2) As a spirit, we no longer have a physical body with flesh and bones; Jesus himself points that out. (Luke 24:39)

3) The dead can unquestionably appear on Earth after they have passed into the spirit world. (Matthew 17:1-13; 1 Sam 28)

4) It is possible – at least under some circumstances – for the living to call the dead back to Earth. (1 Samuel 28)

5) The spirit of the living can leave their bodies in much the same way that happens on death. The spirit can travel about, and see and learn new things. (Ezekiel 8:1-24, and pretty much the entire Book of Revelation)

6) Last, but certainly not least, the Bible is full of strange and wonderful stories, and goes far beyond most people's limited view. Along with ghosts, unicorns, and astral projection, it offers both hope and history to its readers, and some stories and ideas that seem to fly in the face of organized religion today.

Of course, along with these certainties, there are still verses with death threats for those with an interest in the supernatural such as Leviticus 20:27, quoted a couple of times in this book already...

27A man also or woman that hath a familiar spirit, or that is a wizard, shall surely be put to death: they shall stone them with stones: their blood shall be upon them.

As we previously discussed, however, there are many laws that were given in the Bible, for different people at different times. I may never understand why some people work so hard to condemn others using one law, while ignoring all of the others.

The Bible has unfortunately been used as a hammer to judge and condemn people, but I would be fearful to use such a sacred text in that regard. Still, with all of its laws and regulations, the Bible can become quite confusing, and it's easy to get lost in all the minutia.

There has to be a last word on the subject – a

definitive ruling on which laws are important, and which ones are not. And perhaps there is...

A Good Candidate for the Last Word

Perhaps there is no better person – to use the word loosely – to have the last word on the subject than Jesus Himself. It is curious to note that He did supersede Old Testament law while He was on Earth.

Take for example the old "eye for an eye" rule, which is first presented in the Book of Leviticus, Chapter 24, which states:

> [19]*And if a man cause a blemish in his neighbour; as he hath done, so shall it be done to him;*
> [20]*Breach for breach, eye for eye, tooth for tooth: as he hath caused a blemish in a man, so shall it be done to him again.*

Jesus himself commented on this old scripture while giving the famous Sermon on the Mount. This is presented in Matthew 5, which says,

> [38]*Ye have heard that it hath been said, An eye for an eye, and a tooth for a tooth:*
> [39]*But I say unto you, That ye resist not evil: but whosoever shall smite thee on thy right cheek, turn to him the other also.*

Clearly there are laws and ideas in the Old Testament that Jesus revisited, and I'm a big fan of following the teachings of Christ. As shown above, the Old Testament says that if someone puts out your eye, take out his. If someone knocks out your tooth, knock out his. But when Jesus came along, he says that if someone hits your right cheek, turn your left one so that he can hit it as well.

He literally tossed out the Old Testament law on the subject, but then again, I guess that if anyone could do that it would be Him.

When it comes to the various laws of the Bible, however, Christ had something very profound to say. It is recorded in Mark 12:28-31...

[28]And one of the scribes came, and having heard them reasoning together, and perceiving that he had answered them well, asked him, Which is the first commandment of all?

[29]And Jesus answered him, The first of all the commandments is, Hear, O Israel; The Lord our God is one Lord:

[30]And thou shalt love the Lord thy God with all thy heart, and with all thy soul, and with all thy mind, and with all thy strength: this is the first commandment.

[31]And the second is like, namely this, Thou shalt love thy neighbour as thyself. There is none other commandment greater than these.

So while it is simple to find verses in the Bible that condemn any involvement with the supernatural, it's probably not worth arguing whether it's worse to spend a night in a haunted hotel hoping to encounter a spirit, have a romantic tryst with someone of your same gender, or sit down to a dinner of lobster bisque at your favorite seafood restaurant – all definitely are forbidden by specific verses that you can find in the Bible, many of which that we've examined in this book.

Instead, though, when Christ was asked what the greatest law of them all was, you'll notice that his answers all center on love. And when he says to love your neighbor, he doesn't specify only vegetarian neighbors, straight neighbors, or neighbors who aren't interested in the supernatural... but your neighbor, with no judging. And perhaps that's the most important thing that the Bible has to say about ghosts, or pretty much anything else for that matter... and that one truth could very well be the light at the top of the mountain that we all seek.

Index

134